THIS BOOK
BELONGS TO:

Carrie F. Strong

D1402773

THE COMPLETE
MOTHER GOOSE

CHILDREN'S CLASSICS

This unique series of Children's Classics™ features accessible and highly readable texts paired with the work of talented and brilliant illustrators of bygone days to create fine editions for today's parents and children to rediscover and treasure. Besides being a handsome addition to any home library, this series features genuine bonded-leather spines stamped in gold, full-color illustrations, and high-quality acid-free paper that will enable these books to be passed from one generation to the next.

THE COMPLETE
MOTHER GOOSE

WITH ILLUSTRATIONS IN COLOR
AND IN BLACK AND WHITE

BY

E T H E L   F R A N K L I N   B E T T S

PLUS TRADITIONAL DRAWINGS OF
THE NINETEENTH CENTURY

CHILDREN'S CLASSICS

NEW YORK

This 1987 edition is published by Children's Classics, a
division of dilithium Press, Ltd., distributed by Crown
Publishers, Inc., 225 Park Avenue South, New York,
New York 10003.

CHILDREN'S CLASSICS is a trademark of dilithium
Press, Ltd.

Printed and Bound in the United States of America

Library of Congress Cataloging-in-Publication Data

Mother Goose.
    The complete Mother Goose.

    Summary: An illustrated anthology of the
traditional nursery rhymes.
    1. Nursery rhymes.   2. Children's poetry.
[1. Nursery rhymes]   I. Betts, Ethel Franklin, ill.
II. Title.
PZ8.3.M85   1987b   398'.8   86-34310
ISBN 0-517-63383-3 (alk. paper)

h g f e d c b a

Cover design by Clair Moritz

CONTENTS

	PAGE
Foreword	*xxi*
A carrion Crow	122
A curious Discourse	73
A Diller, a Dollar	20
A Frog he would a-wooing go	155
A little cock Sparrow	151
A little old Man and I fell out	214
A Man of Words and not of Deeds . . .	24
A Puzzle	35
A Riddle	133
A Swarm of Bees	210
A Thatcher of Thatchwood	53
A was an Archer	61
All of a Row	220
An Apple Pie	22
Apple-Pie Alphabet	57
As little Jenny Wren	76
As I walked by myself	77
As I was going along, long, long	223
As I was going to sell my Eggs	161

Contents

	PAGE
As I was going to St. Ives	180
As I was going up Pippen Hill	136
As I went through the Garden Gap	223
As soft as Silk	62
As white as Milk	199
Awake, arise, pull out your Eyes	164
Baa, baa, black Sheep	160
Barber, Barber	46
Bat, Bat	51
Bessy Bell and Mary Gray	42
Billy, Billy, come and play	148
Billy Pringle's Pig	116
Bless you, Burny-Bee	124
Blow, Wind, blow! and go, Mill, go!	91
Bobby Shaftoe	136
Bow, wow, wow	209
Bow, wow, says the Dog	45
Brow brinky	215
Buzz and hum	53
Bye, Baby Bunting	22
Charley, Charley	29
Charley Warley	66
Christmas Days	172

Contents

	PAGE
Cock a doodle doo!	137
Cold and raw	213
Come hither	96
Come hither, sweet Robin	217
Come, let's to Bed	2
Come, my Children	164
Come take up your Hats, and away let us haste	63
Cou'd ye?	218
Cross patch	8
Curly Locks	80
Daffy-down-dilly	204
Dance, little Baby	3
Dance to your Daddy	224
Dickery, dickery, dare	203
Diddle, diddle Dumpling	80
Diddle-y-diddle-y-dumpty	212
Ding, dong, bell	100
Ding, dong, darrow	23
Doctor Foster	107
Doodle doodle doo	226
Early to Bed	141
Elizabeth	213
Elsie Marley	150

Contents

	PAGE
F for Fig	90
Fa, la, la, la, lal, de	59
Fiddle cum fee	179
Fiddle-De-Dee	178
Fiddle, faddle, feedle	4
Fire, fire	36
For every Evil under the Sun	17
Formed long ago	154
For want of a Nail	67
Four and twenty Tailors	19
Girls and Boys, come out to play	37
God bless the Master of this House	70
Good People all, of every sort	54
Goosey, Goosey, Gander	60
Great A, little a	191
Gunpowder Treason	101
Gushy Cow bonny	77
Hark! Hark! the Dogs do bark	76
He loves me	163
He that would thrive	7
Hector Protector	33
Here Am I	30
Here goes my Lord	167

Contents

PAGE

Here's Sulky Sue 140

Hey, diddle, diddle 205

Hey-ding-a-ding 217

Hey, dorolot! 116

Hey, my Kitten, my Kitten 87

Hickety, Pickety 189

Hickory dickory dock 208

Higgledy, piggledy 211

High diddle ding 90

Hot-cross Buns! 221

How many Miles? 29

Humpty Dumpty 76

Hush-a-bye, Baby 1

Hush thee, my Babby 3

Hushy Baby, my Doll 50

I do not like thee, Doctor Fell 159

I had a little Dog 191

I had a little Hen 196

I had a little Hobby-horse 98

I had a little Husband 227

I had a little Nut Tree 7

I had a little Pony 75

I have been to Market 199

Contents

	PAGE
I have seen you, little Mouse	46
I like little Pussy	216
I love my Love	17
I saw a Ship a-sailing	13
I saw three Ships come sailing by	6
I will sing you a Song	212
If all the World were Water	38
If I'd as much Money as I could spend	34
If "ifs" and "ands"	227
If Wishes were Horses	154
I'll sing you a Song	167
I'll tell you a Story	201
In a Cottage in Fife	219
In Fir Tar is	135
In marble Walls	11
Intery, mintery, cutery-corn	179
Is John Smith within?	211
Jack and Jill	180
Jack, be nimble	200
Jack Sprat	1
Jack Sprat's Pig	43
Jacky, come give me thy Fiddle	67
January brings the Snow	123

Contents

	PAGE
Jenny Wren	192
Jocky was a Piper's Son	120
John Cook	10
Johnny shall have a new Bonnet	44
Kitty alone and I	102
Ladybug, ladybug	48
Leg over Leg	177
Let us go to the Woods	181
Little Betty Blue	26
Little blue Betty	133
Little Bo-Peep	169
Little Boy Blue	60
Little brown Mouse	190
Little Jack Horner	100
Little jumping Joan	30
Little King Boggen	138
Little Miss Muffet	160
Little Nancy Etticoat	204
Little Polly Flinders	40
Little Robin Redbreast	48
Little Tee Wee	142
Little Tom Twig	99
Little Tommy Tittlemouse	142

Contents

	PAGE
Little Tommy Tucker	198
Little Willie Winkle	138
Lock and Key	147
London Bridge is falling down	149
Long Legs, crooked Thighs	223
Lucy Locket	189
Mary had a pretty Bird	34
Mary, Mary, quite contrary	200
Merry are the Bells	41
Monday alone	197
Monday's Bairn	122
Multiplication is Vexation	14
My Father he died	27
My Lady Wind	5
My little Brother	56
My little old Man and I fell out	226
My Maid Mary	78
My Mammy's Maid	214
Needles and Pins	131
Now we dance, looby, looby, looby	166
Now what do you think?	161
Oh, dear, what can the Matter be?	209
Oh, deary, deary me	134

Contents

		PAGE
Oh, who is so merry	. . . .	72
Old Grimes	. . . .	132
Old King Cole	. . . .	2
Old Mother Hubbard	. . . .	186
Old Woman, old Woman	. . . . .	185
One, he loves	. . . .	91
One-ery, two-ery	. . . .	165
One misty, moisty Morning	. . . . .	220
One old Oxford Ox	. . . .	21
One to make ready	. . . .	99
One, two, buckle my Shoe	. . . . .	121
One, two, three	. . . .	90
One, two, three, four, five	. . . . .	75
Para-mara, dictum, domine	. . . .	105
Pat-a-cake, pat-a-cake	. . . . .	40
Pease Porridge Hot	. . . . . .	204
Peter, Peter, Pumpkin Eater	. . . .	206
Peter Piper	. . . .	119
Pitty Patty Polt	. . . .	22
Playmates	. . . .	101
Polly, put the Kettle on	. . . . .	107
Poor old Robinson Crusoe	. . . .	79
Pussy-cat, Pussy-cat	. . . . . .	20

Contents

	PAGE
Pussy-cat sits by the Fire	190
Pussy sits beside the Fire	87
Rabbit Pie	66
Rain, Rain, go away	89
Ride a Cock-horse to Banbury Cross . . .	200
Ride away	20
Ride, Baby, ride	218
Riddle me, riddle me	16
Ring around a Rosie	130
Robert Barnes, Fellow fine	55
Robert Rowley	26
Robin a-Bobbin	184
Robin Hood	95
Robin the Bobbin	56
Rock-a-bye, Baby	213
Round the Bramble Bush	168
See a Pin and pick it up	214
See, Saw, Margery Daw	40
Shoe the Horse	13
Simple Simon met a Pieman	140
Sing a Song of Six-pence	170
Sing Ivy	15
Sing, sing, what shall I sing?	177
Sing song, merry go round	12

Contents

	PAGE
Six little Mice sat down to spin	4
So, merrily trip and go	215
Solomon Grundy	37
Speak when you're spoken to	163
St. Swithin's Day	147
Taffy was a Welshman	201
Tell-Tale-Tit	26
That's all	206
The Alphabet	111
The Calf, the Goose, the Bee	128
The Cock's on the Housetop	92
The Days of the Month	142
The fat Man of Bombay	132
The Fox and his Wife	194
The House that Jack built	125
The King of France	108
The King of France, and the King of Spain	185
The little Clock	11
The Lion and the Unicorn	39
The Man in the Moon	205
The Man in the Wilderness	23
The North Wind doth blow	14
The old Woman and her Pig	81
The Piper and his Cow	198

Contents

	PAGE
The Queen of Hearts	139
The Rose is red	160
The Song of Five Toes	14
The Spider and the Fly	143
The Toad and the Frog	31
The Way we ride	165
There once were two Cats	92
There was a crooked Man	203
There was a Girl in our Towne	212
There was a jolly Miller	58
There was a little Boy	79
There was a little Guinea-Pig	25
There was a little Man	202
There was a little Man and he woo'd a little Maid	88
There was a mad Man	210
There was a Man, and he had Naught	42
There was a Man, and he was mad	171
There was a Man of our Town	108
There was a Monkey	47
There was an old Man	71
There was an old Man of Tobago	211
There was an old Soldier of Bister	178

Contents

	PAGE
There was an old Woman	31
There was an old Woman	107
There was an old Woman	152
There was an Old Woman	197
There was an old Woman, and what do you think?	38
There was an old Woman of Leeds . . .	224
There was an old Woman sold Puddings and Pies	208
There was an old Woman tossed up in a Basket	202
There were two Blackbirds	18
This is the Death of little Jenny Wren . .	222
This is the Way the Ladies ride	141
Three blind Mice	80
Three Children	19
Three Men in a Tub	209
Three little Kittens	117
Three wise Men of Gotham	16
To Market, to Market	205
Tom, Tom, the Piper's son	180
Tommy Snooks and Betsey Brooks . . .	108
Tommy Trot, a Man of Law	226
Tweedle-Dum and Tweedle-Dee	9

Contents

	PAGE
Twinkle, twinkle, little Star	110
Two little Dogs	99
Two little Kittens	93
Two, three, and four Legs	18
V and I	78
What a fine Bird I be	23
What are little Boys made of?	39
What is the News of the Day?	95
What Shoemaker?	132
When a Twister a twisting	32
When I was a Bachelor	120
When I was a little Girl	129
When good King Arthur ruled this Land	131
When little Fred	43
When the Wind is in the east	9
Where are you going?	221
Where should a Baby rest?	52
Who killed Cock Robin?	68
Why is Pussy in Bed, pray?	225
Willy Boy, where are you going?	161
With a Hop, Step, and a Jump	162
Yankee Doodle	139
Young Lambs to sell	86

ILLUSTRATIONS

IN COLOR

FACING PAGE

A Diller, a Dollar 36

See, Saw, Margery Daw 37

Little Boy Blue 64

Curly Locks 65

Little Jack Horner 94

When I was a Bachelor 95

Simple Simon 124

Little Miss Muffet 125

Jack and Jill 150

Mary, Mary, quite contrary 151

FOREWORD

MOTHER GOOSE is a rich oral heritage for our children; they will find much at which to wonder and rejoice in this book. What child can fail to delight in the rollicking rhythm of

Dickery, dickery, dare,
The pig flew up in the air;
The man in brown soon brought him down,
Dickery, dickery, dare.

Parents who read *Mother Goose* to their children are sure to feel that they are giving a gift of love, for adult and child will share something precious that can never be put into the prose of everyday life.

In this edition, the color illustrations of Ethel Franklin Betts, first published early in this century, perfectly convey the sense that sharing *Mother Goose* is a special experience. Many of her designs draw us into the page, as though we were participants in the scene. For example, looking at her "Little Boy Blue," we experience the sensation of sinking into the fantasies of sleep. Her children inhabit a lyrical, dreamlike world, where flowers unexpectedly appear, contributing to our feeling of a joyous, untouched existence. The artist's use of rich, velvety colors, and her play of designs exhibit the sure touch of a master, as well. This edition also contains line drawings by Ethel Franklin Betts, as well as earlier drawings of the nineteenth century. These latter illustrations, done by different anonymous artists, are rich in characterization and humor—note particularly the hilarious "Old Mother Hubbard" series—and many display a close observation of nature.

Mother Goose rhymes invite joyful participation of child and adult, beginning when the child is still in baby-hood. Picture parents swinging their children to the chant of

> *Dance, little baby, dance up high,*
> *Never mind, baby, mother is by;*
> *Crow and caper, caper and crow,*
> *There, little baby, there you go;*
> *Up to the ceiling, down to the ground,*
> *Backwards and forwards, round and round...*

For the slightly older child, these poems contain the essence of drama in a few well-honed lines, and they invite a child to ask, "Why?" The child wants to know what happened before, and what will happen after the action in the rhyme. Poems such as "There was a jolly miller" or "Old King Cole" also create characters with astonishing economy: images can be haunting, suggesting as much by what is left out as by what is put in. Thus, in

> *Little Willie Winkle runs through the town,*
> *Upstairs and downstairs, in his nightgown,*
> *Rapping at the window, crying through the lock,*
> *"Are the children in their beds? for now it's*
>   *eight o'clock."*

we see Little Willie Winkle, running in the cool of night, his nightgown flapping, flirting with the nighttime's wildness, a child protecting other children. The simple poem of "Hickory, Dickory, Dock" isolates one moment, contrasting the reversibility of human action (portrayed by a mouse), with the ongoingness of time:

> *Hickory, dickory, dock;*
> *The mouse ran up the clock;*
> *The clock struck one,*
> *The mouse ran down,*
> *Hickory, dickory, dock.*

Foreword

Some *Mother Goose* rhymes go from the incomprehensibly large to the comfortably small in just a few lines, as in

> *There was an old woman tossed up in a basket,*
> *Seventy times as high as the moon.*
> *What she did there I could not but ask it,*
> *For in her hand she carried a broom.*
>
> *"Old woman, old woman, old woman," said I,*
> *"Oh whither, oh whither, oh whither so high?"*
> *"To sweep the cobwebs off the sky,*
> *And I shall be back again by and by."*

By hearing the absurd contrasted with the real, the child learns to understand the world at the same time that he begins to question it. In addition, the rhymes are a child's introduction to logic—witness the child's moment of delighted realization of "Why, of course!" in hearing

> *There was an old woman lived under a hill,*
> *And if she's not gone, she lives there still.*

There is pleasure to be had just in the play of sounds—try saying, "Doctor Foster went to Glo'ster." Rhythmical refrains are a happy invitation to join in, as well as pauses to give us time to reinforce a picture in our minds. Some of the poems resound with a sense of celebration, as "I saw three Ships come sailing by." Many of the rhymes are meant to accompany an activity, such as bouncing a baby on a parent's knees, as in "This is the way the Ladies ride"; hand-clapping, as in "Pat-a-cake, pat-a-cake"; or fingerplays, such as "There were two Blackbirds." As children grow a little older, the cumulative stories of "The old Woman and her Pig" and "The House that Jack built" reinforce the child's pleasure in his gradual mastery of the repetition of sequences. And, in addition, themes can be found in the Mother Goose rhymes that the child will later read in folktales. Some of the poems deal with the folly of war, such as "Tweedle-Dum and Tweedle-Dee," who later appeared as characters in *Through the Looking Glass* by Lewis Carroll:

> *Tweedle-dum and Tweedle-dee*
> *Resolved to have a battle,*
> *For Tweedle-dum said Tweedle-dee*
> *Had spoiled his nice new rattle.*

However, adults in past centuries were not so careful of the sensitivities of their children as we are today: there is violence, death, physical punishment, and injury. The wise parent, therefore, will make a judicious choice of what is read to a child.

Hearing Mother Goose, children will thrill to mysterious echoes that also capture the adult reader. These are not only the traces of his own childhood, but beckonings from past centuries as well. Nursery rhymes, as William and Ceil Baring-Gould write in *The Annotated Mother Goose* (Bramhall House, New York, 1962), have roots not only in rhymes created by folk, to accompany children's active games, but also in lullabies, counting-out rhymes, street cries, prayers, drinking and love songs, riddles and "catches," tongue twisters, proverbs, weather lore, and "fragments of ballads commemorating actual occurrences of at least local importance." The Baring-Goulds, quoting Katharine Elwes Thomas in *The Real Personages of Mother Goose* (Lothrop, Lee & Shepard Co., Boston, 1930), also quote scholars who insist the rhymes are "political diatribes, religious philippics, and popular street songs, embodying comedies, tragedies and love episodes of many great historical personages, lavishly interspersed with English and Scotch folklore flung out with dramatic abandon." Whether or not this is true doesn't really matter today.

Foreword

The earliest printed manuscript extant of Mother Goose rhymes is *Tommy Thumb's Pretty Song Book*, printed around 1744 by the London publisher Mary Cooper. It was published in three volumes of small size, but only the second volume now exists, located in the British Museum. Around 1760, John Newbery published *Mother Goose's Melody; or Sonnets for the Cradle*, and it is likely that the Preface was written by Oliver Goldsmith. But the oral tradition of Mother Goose predates these volumes, in some cases by centuries. For the further history of Mother Goose, you are invited to read *The Annotated Mother Goose*, to which I am indebted for factual information.

This present volume contains all the most important poems, and so in this sense can be said to be complete. In truth, no edition can capture all the rhymes, which come, with many variations, from such numerous and diverse sources.

The modern reader may be surprised to discover old-fashioned words and terms and styles of capitalization, but this edition has included these and some of the older variants of the rhymes in order to retain their flavor and quaintness.

Foreword

The Baring-Goulds quote Walter de la Mare who states, in his introduction to *Nursery Rhymes for Certain Times* (Faber & Faber, Ltd., London, 1956), that the Mother Goose rhymes "are tiny masterpieces of word craftsmanship...they are a direct shortcut into poetry itself." The child who, at an early age, has these rhymes read to him will possess a treasure house of remembered delights of story and sound. He will have memories that can only deepen into a love of literature in the years to come.

ELLEN S. SHAPIRO

Brooklyn, New York
1987

Hush-a-bye, Baby.

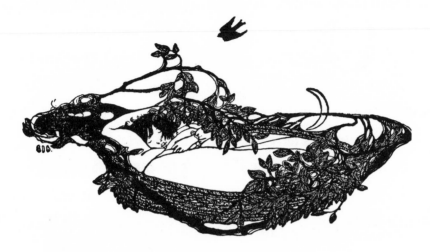

HUSH-A-BYE, baby, on the tree
    top,
When the wind blows, the cradle will
    rock;
When the bough bends the cradle will
    fall,
Down will come baby, bough, cradle, and
    all.

Jack Sprat.

JACK SPRAT could eat no fat,
    His wife could eat no lean;
And so, betwixt them both, [you see]
    They licked the platter clean.

Old King Cole.

OLD King Cole
Was a merry old soul,
And a merry old soul was he;
He called for his pipe,
And he called for his bowl,
And he called for his fiddlers
three.

Every fiddler, he had a fiddle,
And a very fine fiddle had he;
Twee tweedle dee, tweedle dee,
went the fiddlers.
Oh, there's none so rare,
As can compare
With King Cole and his fiddlers
three!

Come, let's to Bed.

COME, let's to bed,
Says Sleepy-head;
Tarry a while, says Slow.
Put on the pan,
Says Greedy Nan,
Let's sup before we go.

Hush thee, my Babby.

HUSH thee, my babby,
  Lie still with thy daddy,
Thy mammy has gone to the mill
  To grind thee some wheat,
  To make thee some meat,
And so, my dear babby, lie still.

Dance, little Baby.

DANCE, little baby, dance up high,
  Never mind, baby, mother is by;
Crow and caper, caper and crow,
There, little baby, there you go;
Up to the ceiling, down to the ground,
Backwards and forwards, round and
    round;
Dance, little baby, and mother will sing,
With the merry coral, ding, ding, ding!

Fiddle, faddle, feedle.

THERE was an owl lived in an oak,
    Wisky, wasky, weedle;
And every word he ever spoke
Was fiddle, faddle, feedle.

A gunner chanced to come that way,
    Wisky, wasky, weedle;
Says he, "I'll shoot you, silly bird,"
    Fiddle, faddle, feedle.

*Six little Mice sat
down to spin.*

SIX little mice sat down to spin,
    Pussy passed by, and she peeped in.
"What are you at, my little men?"
"Making coats for gentlemen."
"Shall I come in and bite off your
    thread?"
"No, no, Miss Pussy, you'll bite off our
    head."

My Lady Wind.

MY lady Wind, my lady Wind,
  Went round about the house to find
    A chink to get her foot in:
She tried the key-hole in the door,
She tried the crevice in the floor,
    And drove the chimney soot in.

And then one night when it was
      dark,
She blew up such a tiny spark,
    That all the house was pothered:
From it she raised up such a flame,
As flamed away to Belting Lane,
    And White Cross folks were
      smothered.

And thus when once, my little dears,
A whisper reaches itching ears,
    The same will come, you'll find:
Take my advice, restrain the tongue,
Remember what old nurse has sung
    Of busy lady Wind!

I saw three Ships
come sailing by.

I SAW three ships come sailing by,
  Sailing by, sailing by,
I saw three ships come sailing by,
  On New-Year's Day in the morning.

And what do you think was in them then,
  In them then, in them then?
And what do you think was in them then,
  On New-Year's Day in the morning.

Three pretty girls were in them then,
  In them then, in them then,
Three pretty girls were in them then,
  On New-Year's Day in the morning.

And one could whistle, and one could sing,
  And one could play on the violin,
Such joy there was at my wedding,
  On New-Year's Day in the morning.

I had a little Nut Tree.

I HAD a little nut tree, nothing
would it bear
But a silver apple and a golden pear;
The King of Spain's daughter came to
see me,
And all for the sake of my little nut tree.
I skipped over water, I danced over sea,
And all the birds in the air couldn't catch
me.

He that would thrive.

HE that would thrive
Must rise at five;
He that hath thriven,
May lie till seven;
And he that by the plough would thrive,
Himself must either hold or drive.

Cross patch.

CROSS patch, draw the latch;
Sit by the fire and spin;
Take a cup and drink it up,
Then call your neighbors in.

8

Tweedle-Dum and Tweedle-Dee.

TWEEDLE-DUM and Tweedle-
dee
Resolved to have a battle,
For Tweedle-dum said Tweedle-dee
Had spoiled his nice new rattle.

Just then flew by a monstrous crow,
As big as a tar barrel,
Which frightened both the heroes so,
They quite forgot their quarrel.

When the Wind is in the east.

WHEN the wind is in the east,
'Tis neither good for man nor
beast;
When the wind is in the north,
The skilful fisher goes not forth;
When the wind is in the south,
It blows the bait in the fishes' mouth;
When the wind is in the west,
Then 'tis at the very best.

9

John Cook.

JOHN COOK had a little grey mare;
　　he, haw, hum!
Her back stood up, and her bones they
　　were bare; he, haw, hum!

John Cook was riding up Shuter's bank;
　　he, haw, hum!
And there his nag did kick and prank;
　　he, haw, hum!

John Cook was riding up Shuter's hill;
　　he, haw, hum!
His mare fell down, and she made her
　　will; he, haw, hum!

The bridle and saddle were laid on the
　　shelf; he, haw, hum!
If you want any more you may sing it
　　yourself; he, haw, hum!

10

The little Clock.

THERE'S a neat little clock,
 In the schoolroom it stands,
And it points to the time
 With its two little hands.

And may we, like the clock,
 Keep a face clean and bright,
With hands ever ready
 To do what is right.

In marble Walls.

IN marble walls as white as milk,
 Lined with a skin as soft as silk;
Within a fountain crystal clear,
A golden apple doth appear.
No doors there are to this stronghold,
Yet thieves break in and steal the gold.

     (*An egg.*)

Sing song, merry go round.

SING song! merry go round,
Here we go up to the moon, oh.
Little Johnnie a penny has found,
And so we'll sing a tune, oh!
What shall I buy?
Johnnie did cry,
With the penny I've found
So bright and round?
What shall you buy?
A kite that will fly
Up to the moon, all through the sky!
But if, when it gets there,
It should stay in the air.
Or the man in the moon
Should open the door,
And take it in with his long, long paw,—
We should sing to another tune, oh!

I saw a Ship a-sailing.

I SAW a ship a-sailing,
  A-sailing on the sea;
And it was full of pretty things
  For baby and for me.

There were comfits in the cabin,
  And apples in the hold;
The sails were all of velvet,
  And the masts of beaten gold.

The four-and-twenty sailors
  That stood between the decks,
Were four-and-twenty white mice,
  With chains about their necks.

The captain was a duck,
  With a packet on his back;
And when the ship began to move,
  The captain said, "Quack! quack!"

———

Shoe the horse, and shoe the mare;
But let the little colt go bare.

The North Wind doth blow.

THE north wind doth blow,
And we shall have snow,
And what will poor Robin do then?
Poor thing!

He'll sit in a barn,
And to keep himself warm,
Will hide his head under his wing.
Poor thing!

The Song of five Toes.

1. This little pig went to market;
2. This little pig stayed at home;
3. This little pig had roast beef;
4. This little pig had none;
5. This little pig said, wee, wee, wee!
I can't find my way home.

Multiplication is Vexation.

MULTIPLICATION is vexation,
Division is just as bad;
The Rule of Three perplexes me,
And Practice drives me mad.

Sing Ivy.

MY father left me three acres of land,
    Sing ivy, sing ivy;
My father left me three acres of land,
    Sing holly, go whistle and ivy!

I ploughed it with a ram's horn,
    Sing ivy, sing ivy;
And sowed it all over with one pepper-
    corn,
    Sing holly, go whistle and ivy!

I harrowed it with a bramble bush,
    Sing ivy, sing ivy;
And reaped it with my little penknife,
    Sing holly, go whistle, and ivy!

I got the mice to carry it to the barn,
    Sing ivy, sing ivy;
And thrashed it with a goose's quill,
    Sing holly, go whistle, and ivy!

Sing Ivy.

I got the cat to carry it to the mill,
　　Sing ivy, sing ivy;
The miller he swore he would have her
　　paw,
And the cat she swore she would scratch
　　his face,
　　Sing holly, go whistle, and ivy!

RIDDLE-ME, riddle-me, riddle-me-
　　ree,
Perhaps you can tell what this riddle may
　　be:
As deep as a house, as round as a cup,
And all the King's horses can't draw it
　　up.　　　　　　　　　　(*A well.*)

Three wise Men of Gotham.

THREE wise men of Gotham
　　Went to sea in a bowl.
If the bowl had been stronger,
My song had been longer.

For every Evil under
the Sun.

FOR every evil under the sun,

There is a remedy, or there is none,

If there be one, seek till you find it;

If there be none, never mind it.

I love my Love.

I LOVE my love with an A, because

he's Agreeable.

I hate him because he's Avaricious.

He took me to the Sign of the Acorn,

And treated me with Apples.

His name's Andrew,

And he lives at Arlington.

(*This can be continued through the al-*
phabet.)

17

There were two Blackbirds.

THERE were two blackbirds
    Sitting on a hill,
The one named Jack,
    The other named Jill;
Fly away, Jack!
Fly away, Jill!
Come again, Jack!
Come again, Jill!

Two, three, and four Legs.

TWO legs sat upon three legs,
    With one leg in his lap;
In comes four legs,
And runs away with one leg.
Up jumps two legs,
Catches up three legs,
Throws it after four legs,
And makes him bring back one leg.

Three Children.

THREE children sliding on the ice
    Upon a summer's day,
It so fell out, they all fell in,
    The rest they ran away.

Now had these children been at home,
    Or sliding on dry ground,
Ten thousand pounds to one penny
    They had not all been drown'd.

You parents all that children have,
    And you that have got none,
If you would have them safe abroad,
    Pray keep them safe at home.

Four and twenty Tailors.

FOUR and twenty tailors went to kill
    a snail,
The best man among them durst not touch
    her tail;
She put out her horns like a little Kyloe
    cow,
Run, tailors, run, or she'll kill you all
    e'en now.

19

Pussy-cat, Pussy-cat.

PUSSY-CAT, pussy-cat, where have
you been?
I've been up to London to look at the
queen.
Pussy-cat, pussy-cat, what did you there?
I frightened a little mouse under the
chair.

A Diller, a Dollar.

A DILLER, a dollar,
A ten o'clock scholar,
What makes you come so soon?
You used to come at ten o'clock,
But now you come at noon.

Ride away.

RIDE away, ride away, Johnny shall
ride,
And he shall have pussy-cat tied to one
side;
And he shall have little dog tied to the
other;
And Johnny shall ride to see his grandmother.

One old Oxford Ox.

ONE old Oxford ox opening oysters;
    Two tee-totums totally tired of try-
      ing to trot to Tedsbury;
Three thick thumping tigers tickling
    trout;
Four fat friars fanning fainting flies;
Five frippy Frenchmen foolishly fishing
    for flies;
Six sportsmen shooting snipes;
Seven Severn salmons swallowing
    shrimps;
Eight Englishmen eagerly examining
    Europe;
Nine nimble noblemen nibbling nonpa-
    reils;
Ten tinkers tinkling upon ten tin tinder-
    boxes with ten tenpenny tacks;
Eleven elephants elegantly equipt;
Twelve typographical topographers
    typically translating types.

An Apple Pie.

AN apple pie, when it looks nice,
Would make one long to have a
slice,
But if the taste should prove so, too,
I fear one slice would scarcely do.
So to prevent my asking twice,
Pray, mamma, cut a good large slice.

Pitty Patty Polt.

PITTY Patty Polt,
Shoe the wild colt!
Here a nail, and there a nail,
Pitty Patty Polt.

Bye, Baby Bunting.

BYE, Baby Bunting,
Father's gone a hunting,
To get a little rabbit skin
To wrap the Baby Bunting in.

The Man in the Wilderness.

THE man in the wilderness asked me,
How many strawberries grew in
the sea?
I answered him, as I thought good,
As many as red herrings grew in the
wood.

Ding, dong, darrow.

DING, dong, darrow,
The cat and the sparrow;
The little dog has burnt his tail,
And he shall be hanged to-morrow.

What a fine Bird I be.

RIDDLE me, riddle me, ree,
A hawk sate up on a tree;
And he says to himself, says he,
Oh dear! what a fine bird I be!

*A Man of Words and
not of Deeds.*

A MAN of words and not of deeds,

Is like a garden full of weeds;

And when the weeds begin to grow,

It's like a garden full of snow;

And when the snow begins to fall,

It's like a bird upon the wall;

And when the bird away does fly,

It's like an eagle in the sky;

And when the sky begins to roar,

It's like a lion at the door;

And when the door begins to crack,

It's like a stick across your back;

And when your back begins to
smart,

It's like a penknife in your heart;

And when your heart begins to
bleed,

You're dead, and dead, and dead,
indeed.

There was a little
Guinea-Pig.

THERE was a little Guinea-pig,
Who, being little, was not big;
He always walked upon his feet,
And never fasted when he eat.

When from a place he ran away,
He never at that place did stay;
And while he ran, as I am told,
He ne'er stood still for young or old.

He often squeak'd and sometimes vi'lent,
And when he squeak'd he ne'er was silent;
Though ne'er instructed by a cat,
He knew a mouse was not a rat.

One day, as I am certified,
He took a whim and fairly died;
And, as I'm told by men of sense,
He never has been living since.

Robert Rowley.

ROBERT ROWLEY rolled a round
    roll round,
A round roll Robert Rowley rolled
    round;
Where rolled the round roll Robert Row-
    ley rolled round?

Little Betty Blue.

LITTLE Betty Blue
Lost her holiday shoe.
    What shall little Betty do?
    Buy her another
    To match the other,
And then she'll walk in two.

Tell-Tale-Tit.

TELL-TALE-TIT,
    Your tongue shall be slit,
And all the little puppy dogs
Shall have a little bit.

My Father he died.

MY father he died, but I can't tell you
how,

He left me six horses to drive in my

plough:

With my wing wang waddle oh,

Jack sing saddle oh,

Blowsey boys buble oh,

Under the broom.

I sold my six horses, and I bought me a

cow,

I'd fain have made a fortune, but did not

know how:

With my wing wang waddle oh,

Jack sing saddle oh,

Blowsey boys buble oh,

Under the broom.

My Father he died.

I sold my cow, and I bought me a calf;

I'd fain have made a fortune, but lost the

best half;

With my wing wang waddle oh,

Jack sing saddle oh,

Blowsey boys buble oh,

Under the broom.

I sold my calf, and I bought me a cat;

A pretty thing she was, in my chimney

corner sat:

With my wing wang waddle oh,

Jack sing saddle oh,

Blowsey boys buble oh,

Under the broom.

I sold my cat, and bought me a mouse;

He carried fire in his tail, and burnt down

my house:

My Father he died.

With my wing wang waddle oh,
Jack sing saddle oh,
Blowsey boys buble oh,
Under the broom.

How many Miles?

HOW many miles is it to Babylon?—
Threescore miles and ten.
Can I get there by candle-light?—
Yes, and back again!
If your heels are nimble and light,
You may get there by candle-light.

Charley, Charley.

CHARLEY, Charley, stole the barley
Out of the baker's shop;
The baker came out, and gave him a clout,
And made poor Charley hop.

ᚻERE am I, little jumping Joan;
When nobody's with me, I'm always alone.

"CROAK!" said the Toad, "I'm hungry, I think,
To-day I've had nothing to eat or to drink;
I'll crawl to a garden and jump through the pales,
And there I'll dine nicely on slugs and on snails."
"Ho, ho!" quoth the Frog, "is that what you mean?
Then I'll hop away to the next meadow stream,
There I will drink, and eat worms and slugs too,
And then I shall have a good dinner like you."

There was an old woman lived under a hill,
And if she's not gone, she lives there still.

WHEN a Twister a twisting, will twist
    him a twist;
For the twisting of his twist, he
    three times doth intwist;
But if one of the twines of the twist
    do untwist,
The twine that untwisteth, untwist-
    eth the twist.

Untwirling the twine that untwist-
    eth between,
He twirls, with the twister, the two
    in a twine:
Then twice having twisted the
    twines of the twine,
He twisteth the twine he had twined
    in twain.

When a Twister
a twisting.

> The twain that, in twining, before
> > in the twine,
>
> As twines were intwisted; he now
> > doth untwine:
>
> 'Twixt the twain inter-twisting **a**
> > twine more between,
>
> **He,** twirling his twister, makes **a**
> > twist of the twine.

Hector Protector.

HECTOR PROTECTOR was
dressed all in green;
Hector Protector was sent to the Queen.
The Queen did not like him,
No more did the King:
So Hector Protector was sent back again.

If I'd as much Money
as I could spend.

IF I'd as much money as I could
    spend,
I never would cry old chairs to mend;
Old chairs to mend, old chairs to mend;
I never would cry old chairs to mend.
If I'd as much money as I could tell,
I never would cry old clothes to sell;
Old clothes to sell, old clothes to sell;
I never would cry old clothes to sell.

Mary had a pretty Bird.

MARY had a pretty bird,
    Feathers bright and yellow;
Slender legs, upon my word,
    He was a pretty fellow.
The sweetest notes he always sung,
    Which much delighted Mary;
And near the cage she'd ever sit,
    To hear her own canary.

34

A Puzzle.

HAVE you seen the old woman of
Banbury Cross,
Who rode to the fair on the top of her
horse?
And since her return she still tells, up and
down,
Of the wonderful lady she saw when in
town.
She has a small mirror in each of her
eyes,
And her nose is a bellows of minnikin
size;
There's a neat little drum fix'd in each of
her ears,
Which beats a tattoo to whatever she
hears.
She has in each jaw a fine ivory mill,
And day after day she keeps grinding it
still.
Both an organ and flute in her small
throat are placed,

A Puzzle.

And they are played by a steam engine
worked in her breast.

But the wonder of all, in her mouth it is
said,

She keeps a loud bell that might waken
the dead;

And so frightened the woman, and star-
tled the horse,

That they galloped full speed back to
Banbury Cross.

Fire, fire.

FIRE! fire!" said the town crier;
"Where? where?" said Goody
Blair;

"Down the town," said Goody Brown;

"I'll go and see 't," said Goody Fleet;

"So will I," said Goody Fry.

36

A Diller, a Dollar.
Page 20

See Saw, Margery Daw.
Page 40

Girls and Boys, come out to play.

GIRLS and boys, come out to play,
The moon doth shine as bright as day
Leave your supper, and leave your sleep,
And come with your playfellows into the
    street,
Come with a whoop, come with a call,
Come with a good will or not at all.
Up the ladder and down the wall,
A halfpenny roll will serve us all;
You find milk, and I'll find flour,
And we'll have a pudding in half-an-hour.

Solomon Grundy.

SOLOMON GRUNDY,
Born on a Monday,
Christened on Tuesday,
Married on Wednesday,
Took ill on Thursday,
Worse on Friday,
Died on Saturday,
Buried on Sunday:
This is the end
Of Solomon Grundy.

There was an old Woman,
and what do you think?

THERE was an old woman, and what
do you think?
She lived upon nothing but victuals and
drink:
Victuals and drink were the chief of her
diet;
Yet this little old woman could never keep
quiet.

She went to the baker, to buy her some
bread,
And when she came home her old husband
was dead;
She went to the clerk to toll the bell,
And when she came back her old husband
was well.

If all the World were Water.

IF all the world were water,
And all the sea were ink,
What should we do for bread and cheese?
What should we do for drink?

What are little Boys made of?

WHAT are little boys made of, made
     of,
What are little boys made of?
Snaps and snails, and puppydog's tails;
And that's what little boys are made of,
    made of.

What are little girls made of, made of,
    made of,
What are little girls made of?
Sugar and spice, and all that's nice;
And that's what little girls are made of,
    made of.

The Lion and the Unicorn.

THE lion and the unicorn
    Were fighting for the crown;
The lion beat the unicorn
    All round about the town.
Some gave them white bread,
    And some gave them brown;
Some gave them plum-cake,
    And sent them out of town.

See, Saw, Margery Daw.

SEE, Saw, Margery Daw,
Sold her bed and lay upon straw;
Was not she a dirty slut,
To sell her bed and lie in the dirt!
Great A, little a, Bouncing B,
The cat's in the cupboard, and she can't
see.

Little Polly Flinders.

LITTLE Polly Flinders
Sat among the cinders,
Warming her pretty little toes!
Her mother came and caught her,
And whipped her little daughter,
For spoiling her nice new clothes.

Pat-a-cake, pat-a-cake.

PAT-A-CAKE, pat-a-cake, baker's man!
Make me a cake, as fast as you can:
Pat it, and prick it, and mark it with T,
Put it in the oven for Tommy and me.

Merry are the Bells.

MERRY are the bells, and merry
would they ring,
Merry was myself, and merry could I
sing;
With a merry ding-dong, happy, gay, and
free,
And a merry sing-song, happy let us be!

Waddle goes your gait, and hollow are
your hose,
Noddle goes your pate, and purple is
your nose;
Merry is your sing-song, happy, gay, and
free,
With a merry ding-dong, happy let us
be!

Merry have we met, and merry have we
been,
Merry let us part, and merry meet again;
With our merry sing-song, happy, gay,
and free,
And a merry ding-dong, happy let us
be!

There was a Man, and
he had Naught.

THERE was a man, and he had
naught,
  And robbers came to rob him;
He crept up to the chimney pot,
  And then they thought they had him.

But he got down on t'other side,
  And then they could not find him;
He ran fourteen miles in fifteen days,
  And never looked behind him.

Bessy Bell and Mary Gray.

BESSY BELL and Mary Gray,
  They were two bonny lasses:
They built their house upon the lea,
  And covered it with rashes.

Bessy kept the garden gate,
  And Mary kept the pantry:
Bessy always had to wait,
  While Mary lived in plenty.

When little Fred.

WHEN little Fred
Was called to bed,
He always acted right;
He kissed Mamma,
And then Papa,
And wished them all good-night.

He made no noise,
Like naughty boys,
But gently upstairs
Directly went,
When he was sent,
And always said his prayers.

Jack Sprat's Pig.

JACK SPRAT'S pig,
He was not very little,
Nor yet very big;
He was not very lean,
He was not very fat;
He'll do well for a grunt,
Says little Jack Sprat.

JOHNNY shall have a new bonnet,
  And Johnny shall go to the fair,
And Johnny shall have a blue ribbon
  To tie up his bonny brown hair.
And why may not I love Johnny?
  And why may not Johnny love me?
And why may not I love Johnny
  As well as another body?

And here's a leg for a stocking,
  And here is a leg for a shoe,
And he has a kiss for his daddy,
  And two for his mammy, I trow.
And why may not I love Johnny?
  And why may not Johnny love me?
And why may not I love Johnny,
  As well as another body?

Bow, wow, says the Dog.

BOW, wow, says the dog;
  Mew, mew, says the cat;
Grunt, grunt, goes the hog;
  And squeak goes the rat.

Chirp, chirp, says the sparrow;
  Caw, caw, says the crow;
Quack, quack, says the duck;
  And what cuckoos say, you know.

So, with sparrows and cuckoos;
  With rats and with dogs;
With ducks and with crows;
  With cats and with hogs;

A fine song I have made,
  To please you, my dear;
And if it's well sung,
  'Twill be charming to hear.

I have seen you, little Mouse.

I HAVE seen you, little mouse,
Running all about the house,
Through the hole, your little eye
In the wainscot peeping sly,
Hoping soon some crumbs to steal,
To make quite a hearty meal.
Look before you venture out,
See if pussy is about,
If she's gone, you'll quickly run,
To the larder for some fun,
Round about the dishes creep,
Taking into each a peep,
To choose the daintiest that's there,
Spoiling things you do not care.

Barber, Barber.

BARBER, barber, shave a pig,
How many hairs will make a wig?
" Four and twenty, that's enough."
Give the barber a pinch of snuff.

There was a Monkey.

THERE was a monkey climb'd up a
   tree,
When he fell down, then down fell he.

There was a crow sat on a stone,
When he was gone, then there was none.

There was an old wife did eat an apple,
When she had ate two, she had ate a
   couple.

There was a horse going to the mill,
When he went on, he stood not still.

There was a butcher cut his thumb
When it did bleed, then blood did come.

There was a lackey ran a race,
When he ran fast, he ran apace.

There was a cobbler clowting shoon,
When they were mended, they were done.

There was a chandler making candle,
When he them strip, he did them handle.

There was a navy went into Spain,
When it return'd, it came again.

Ladybug, ladybug.

LADYBUG, ladybug,
Fly away home,
Your house is on fire,
And your children will burn.

Little Robin Redbreast.

LITTLE Robin Redbreast sat upon
a tree,
Up went Pussy cat, and down went he;
Down came Pussy cat, and away Robin
ran;
Says little Robin Redbreast, "Catch me
if you can."
Little Robin Redbreast jump'd upon a
wall,
Pussy cat jump'd after him, and almost
got a fall,
Little Robin chirp'd and sang, and what
did Pussy say?
Pussy cat said "Mew," and Robin jump'd
away.

48

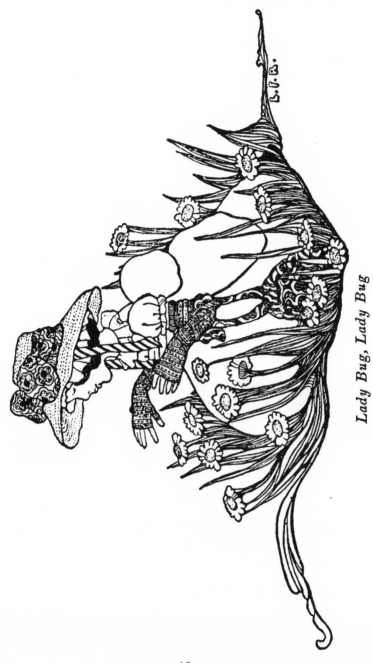

Lady Bug, Lady Bug

Hushy Baby, my Doll.

HUSHY baby, my doll, I pray you
don't cry,

And I'll give you some bread and some
milk by-and-by;

Or, perhaps you like custard, or maybe
a tart,—

Then to either you're welcome, with all
my whole heart.

But how, my dear baby, shall I make you
eat

Of the bread, or the milk, or the custard,
or meat?

For those pretty red lips seem shut up so
fast,

I much fear they won't open to taste the
repast.

Hushy Baby, my Doll.

Ah! but then, my sweet child, you'll surely

not cry,

Oh no, not one tear is there now in your

eye;

Come kiss me, my dear, then, although

you're but wood,

For I'm sure now you smile, and look

very good.

Bat, Bat.

BAT, bat,

Come under my hat,

And I'll give you a slice of bacon;

And when I bake,

I'll give you a cake,

If I am not mistaken.

Where should a
Baby rest?

WHERE should a baby rest?
Where but on its mother's arm —
Where can a baby lie
Half so safe from every harm?
Lulla, lulla, lullaby,
Softly sleep, my baby;
Lulla, lulla, lullaby,
Soft, soft, my baby.

Nestle there, my lovely one!
Press to mine thy velvet cheek;
Sweetly coo, and smile, and look,
All the love thou canst not speak.
Lulla, lulla, lullaby,
Softly sleep, my baby;
Lulla, lulla, lullaby,
Soft, soft, my baby.

Buzz and hum.

BUZZ, quoth the blue fly,

Hum, quoth the bee,

Buzz and hum they cry,

And so do we:

In his ear, in his nose, thus, do you see?

He ate the dormouse, else it was he.

A Thatcher of Thatchwood.

A THATCHER of Thatchwood

went to Thatchet a-thatching;

Did a thatcher of Thatchwood go to

Thatchet a-thatching?

If a thatcher of Thatchwood went to

Thatchet a-thatching,

Where's the thatching the thatcher of

Thatchwood has thatched?

Good People all, of every sort.

GOOD people all, of every sort,
 Give ear unto my song:
And if you find it wondrous short,
 It cannot hold you long.

In Islington there was a man,
 Of whom the world might say,
That still a Godly race he ran,
 Whene'er he went to pray.

A kind and gentle heart he had,
 To comfort friends and foes;
The naked every day he clad,
 When he put on his clothes.

And in that town a dog was found:
 As many dogs there be—
Both mongrel, puppy, whelp, and hound,
 And curs of low degree.

This dog and man at first were friends,
 But, when a pique began,
The dog, to gain some private ends,
 Went mad, and bit the man.

Good People all, of every sort.

Around from all the neighbouring streets
    The wondering neighbours ran;
And swore the dog had lost his wits,
    To bite so good a man.

The wound it seemed both sore and sad
    To every Christian eye;
And while they swore the dog was mad,
    They swore the man would die.

But soon a wonder came to light,
    That showed the rogues they lied—
The man recovered of the bite;
    The dog it was that died.

Robert Barnes, Fellow fine.

ROBERT BARNES, fellow fine,
    Can you shoe this horse of mine?"
"Yes, good Sir, that I can,
As well as any other man;
There's a nail, and there's a prod,
And now, good Sir, your horse is shod."

Robin the Bobbin.

ROBIN the Bobbin, the big bouncing
Ben,
He ate more meat than fourscore men;
He ate a cow, he ate a calf,
He ate a butcher and a half;
He ate a church, he ate a steeple,
He ate the priest and all the people!

My little Brother.

I LOVE you well, my little brother,
And you are fond of me;
Let us be kind to one another,
As brothers ought to be.
You shall learn to play with me,
And learn to use my toys;
And then I think that we shall be
Two happy little boys.

Apple-Pie Alphabet.

A was an apple-pie;

B bit it;

C cut it;

D dealt it;

E eat it;

F fought for it;

G got it;

H had it;

J joined it;

K kept it;

L longed for it;

M mourned for it;

N nodded at it;

O opened it;

P peeped in it;

Q quartered it;

57

Apple-Pie Alphabet.

R ran for it;

S stole it;

T took it;

V viewed it;

W wanted it;

X Y, and Z all wished a piece of it.

There was a jolly Miller.

THERE was a jolly miller
  Lived on the river Dee:
He worked and sang from morn till night,
 No lark so blithe as he,
And this the burden of his song
 For ever used to be—
"I jump mejerrime jee!
 I care for nobody—no! not I,
Since nobody cares for me."

58

Apple-Pie Alphabet.
Page 57

Apple-Pie Alphabet.
Page 58

Fa, la, la, la, lal, de.

THERE were two birds sat on a
        stone,
    Fa, la, la, la, lal, de;
One flew away and then there was one,
    Fa, la, la, la, lal, de;
The other flew after, and then there was
        none,
    Fa, la, la, la, lal, de;
And so the poor stone was left all alone,
    Fa, la, la, la, lal, de!

Of these two birds one back again flew,
    Fa, la, la, la, lal, de;
The other came after, and then there were
        two,
    Fa, la, la, la, lal, de;
Said one to the other,
        "Pray how do you do?"
    Fa, la, la, la, lal, de;
"Very well, thank you, and pray how
        do you?"
    Fa, la, la, la, lal; de!

Little Boy Blue.

LITTLE Boy Blue, go blow your
horn,
The sheep's in the meadow, the cow's in
the corn.
Where's the little boy, that tends the
sheep?
He's under the haycock fast asleep.

Goosey, Goosey, Gander.

GOOSEY, goosey, gander,
Where dost thou wander?
Up stairs and down stairs,
And in my lady's chamber.
There I met an old man
Who would not say his prayers,
I took him by the hind legs
And threw him down stairs.

60

There was a jolly Miller.
Page 58

Little Boy Blue.
Page 60

A was an Archer.

A was an archer, and shot at a frog,

B was a butcher, and had a great dog.

C was a captain, all covered with lace,

D was a drunkard, and had a red face.

E was an esquire, with pride on his brow,

F was a farmer, and followed the plough.

G was a gamester, who had but ill luck,

H was a hunter, and hunted a buck.

I was an innkeeper, who loved to bouse,

J was a joiner, and built up a house.

K was King William, once governed this
      land,

L was a lady, who had a white hand.

M was a miser, and hoarded up gold,

N was a nobleman, gallant and bold.

O was an oyster wench, and went about
      town,

A was an Archer.

P was a parson, and wore a black gown.

Q was a queen, who was fond of good flip,

R was a robber, and wanted a whip.

S was a sailor, and spent all he got,

T was a tinker, and mended a pot.

U was an usurer, a miserable elf,

V was a vintner, who drank all himself.

W was a watchman, and guarded the door,

X was expensive, and so became poor.

Y was a youth, that did not love school,

Z was a zany, a poor harmless fool.

As soft as Silk.

As soft as silk, as white as milk,
As bitter as gall, a strong wall,
And a green coat covers me all.

(*A walnut.*)

COME take up your hats, and away
      let us haste,
To the Butterfly's Ball, and the Grass-
      hopper's Feast.
The trumpeter, Gad-fly, has summoned
      the crew,
And the revels are now only waiting for
      you.

On the smooth shaven grass, by the side
      of a wood,
Beneath a broad oak which for ages had
      stood,
See the children of earth, and the tenants
      of air,
To an evening's amusement together re-
      pair.

And there came the Beetle so blind and
      so black,

Come take up your Hats,
and away let us haste.

> Who carried the Emmet, his friend, on
> his back.
> And there came the Gnat and the
> Dragon-fly too,
> With all their relations, green, orange,
> and blue.

> And there came the Moth, with her plum-
> age of down,
> And the Hornet with jacket of yellow and
> brown;
> And with him the Wasp, his companion,
> did bring,
> But they promised that evening to lay by
> their sting.

> Then the sly little Dormouse peeped out
> of his hole,
> And led to the Feast his blind cousin the
> Mole:

Little Boy Blue.
Page 60

Curly Locks.
Page 80

Come take up your Hats,
and away let us haste.

And the Snail, with her horns peeping out
of her shell,
Came, fatigued with the distance, the
length of an ell.

A mushroom the table, and on it was
spread
A water-dock leaf, which their table-cloth
made.
The viands were various, to each of their
taste,
And the Bee brought the honey to sweeten
the feast.

With steps most majestic the Snail did
advance,
And he promised the gazers a minuet to
dance;
But they all laughed so loud that he drew
in his head,
And went in his own little chamber to
bed.

Come take up your Hats,
and away let us haste.

Then, as evening gave way to the shadows
of night,
Their watchman, the Glow-worm, came
out with his light.
So home let us hasten, while yet we can
see,
For no watchman is waiting for you or
for me.

Charley Warley.

CHARLEY WARLEY had a cow,
Black and white about the brow;
Open the gate and let her go through,
Charley Warley's old cow!

RABBIT, Rabbit, Rabbit Pie!
Come, my ladies, come and buy;
Else your babies they will cry.

66

For want of a Nail.

FOR want of a nail, the shoe was lost,
   For want of the shoe, the horse was
     lost,
For want of the horse, the rider was lost,
For want of the rider, the battle was lost,
For want of the battle, the kingdom was
     lost,
   And all from the want of a horseshoe
     nail!

*Jacky, come give
me thy Fiddle.*

JACKY, come give me thy fiddle,
   If ever thou mean to thrive.
Nay; I'll not give my fiddle
   To any man alive.

If I should give my fiddle,
   They'll think that I'm gone mad;
For many a joyful day
   My fiddle and I have had.

Who killed Cock Robin?

WHO killed Cock Robin?
  "I," said the sparrow,
  "With my bow and arrow,
I killed Cock Robin."

Who saw him die?
  "I," said the fly,
  "With my little eye,
I saw him die."

Who caught his blood?
  "I," said the fish,
  "With my little dish,
I caught his blood."

Who'll make his shroud?
  "I," said the beetle,
  "With my thread and needle,
I'll make his shroud."

Who'll bear the torch?
  "I," the linnet,
  "Will come in a minute,
I'll bear the torch."

Who killed Cock Robin?
Page 68

Who killed Cock Robin?
Page 70

Who killed Cock Robin?

Who'll be the clerk?
  " I," said the lark,
  " I'll say Amen in the dark,
I'll be the clerk."

Who'll dig his grave?
  " I," said the owl,
  "With my spade and shovel,
I'll dig his grave."

Who'll be the parson?
  " I," said the rook,
  " With my little book,
I'll be the parson."

Who'll be chief mourner?
  " I," said the dove,
  "I mourn for my love,
I'll be chief mourner."

Who'll sing his dirge?
  " I," said the thrush,
  " As I sing in a bush,
I'll sing his dirge."

Who killed Cock Robin?

Who'll carry his coffin?
   " I," said the kite,
   " If it be in the night,
I'll carry his coffin."

Who'll toll the bell?
   " I," said the bull,
   " Because I can pull,
I'll toll the bell."

All the birds of the air
   Fell sighing and sobbing,
When they heard the bell toll
   For poor Cock Robin.

God bless the Master of this House.

GOD bless the master of this house,
   The mistress bless also,
And all the little children
   That round the table go;
And all your kin and kinsmen,
   That dwell both far and near:
I wish you a merry Christmas,
   And a happy new year.

70

There was an old Man.

THERE was an old man who lived in
 a wood,
  As you may plainly see;
He said he could do as much work in a
  day
  As his wife could do in three.

"With all my heart," the old woman said;
  "If that you will allow,
To-morrow you'll stay at home in my
  stead,
  And I'll go drive the plough;

But you must milk the Tidy cow,
  For fear that she go dry;
And you must feed the little pigs
  That are within the stye;

And you must mind the speckled hen,
  For fear she lay away;
And you must reel the spool of yarn
  That I span yesterday."

Oh, who is so merry.

OH, who is so merry, so merry, heigh
    ho!
As the light-hearted fairy, heigh ho! heigh
    ho!
    He dances and sings
    To the sound of his wings,
With a hey and a heigh and a ho!

Oh, who is so merry, so airy, heigh ho!
As the light-hearted fairy, heigh ho! heigh
    ho!
    His nectar he sips
    From a primrose's lips,
With a hey and a heigh and a ho!

Oh, who is so merry, so merry, heigh ho!
As the light-footed fairy, heigh ho! heigh
    ho!
    His night is the noon
    And his sun is the moon,
With a hey and a heigh and a ho!

A curious Discourse.

A CURIOUS discourse about an Apple-pie, that passed between the Twenty-five Letters at Dinner-time.

Says A, Give me a good large slice.

Says B, A little Bit, but nice.

Says C, Cut me a piece of Crust.

Says D, It is as Dry as Dust.

Says E, I'll Eat now, fast who will.

Says F, I vow I'll have my Fill.

Says G, Give it to me Good and Great.

Says H, A little bit I Hate.

Says I, I love the Juice the best.

And K the very same confessed.

Says L, There's nothing more I Love.

A curious Discourse.

Says M, it makes your teeth to Move.

N Noticed what the others said.

O Others' plates with grief surveyed.

P Praised the cook up to the life.

Q Quarrelled 'cause he'd a bad knife.

Says R, It Runs short, I'm afraid.

S Silent sat, and nothing said.

T thought that Talking might lose time.

U Understood it at meals a crime.

W Wished there had been a quince in.

Says X, Those cooks there's no convinc-
   ing.

Says Y, I'll eat, let others wish.

Z sat as mute as any fish.

While ampersand, he licked the dish.

I had a little Pony.

I HAD a little pony,
They called him Dapple Grey,
I lent him to a lady,
To ride a mile away.

She whipped him, she lashed him,
She drove him through the mire,
I wadna gie my pony yet
For all the lady's hire.

One, two, three, four, five.

ONE, two, three, four, five,
    I have caught a fish alive;
Six, seven, eight, nine, ten,
I have let it go again.
Why did you let it go?
Because it bit my finger so.
Which finger did it bite?
The little one on the right.

As little Jenny Wren.

AS little Jenny Wren
Was sitting by the shed,
She waggled with her tail,
And nodded with her head.
She waggled with her tail,
And nodded with her head,
As little Jenny Wren
Was sitting by the shed.

Hark! Hark! the Dogs do bark.

HARK! Hark! the dogs do bark,
The beggars have come to town;
Some in rags, and some in tags,
And some in velvet gowns.

Humpty Dumpty.

HUMPTY DUMPTY sat on a wall,
Humpty Dumpty had a great fall,
Threescore men and threescore more
Cannot place Humpty Dumpty as he
was before.

As I walked by myself.

AS I walked by myself,
I talked to myself,
And the self-same self said to me,
Look out for thyself,
Take care of thyself,
For nobody cares for thee.
I answered myself,
And said to myself
In the self-same repartee,
Look to thyself,
Or not look to thyself,
The self-same thing will be.

Gushy Cow bonny.

GUSHY cow bonny,
Let down thy milk,
And I will give thee a gown of silk;
A gown of silk and a silver tee,
If thou wilt let down thy milk to me.

V and I.

WHEN V and I together meet,
They make the number Six complete.
When I with V doth meet once more,
Then 'tis they Two can make but Four.
And when that V from I is gone
Alas! poor I can make but One.

My Maid Mary.

MY maid Mary she minds her dairy,
While I go a-hoeing and mowing each morn;
Merrily run the reel and the little spinning-wheel
Whilst I am singing and mowing my corn.

Poor old Robinson Crusoe.

POOR old Robinson Crusoe!
Poor old Robinson Crusoe!
They made him a coat
Of an old nanny goat,
   I wonder how they could do so!
With a ring a ting tang,
And a ring a ting tang,
   Poor old Robinson Crusoe!

There was a little Boy.

THERE was a little boy and a little
    girl
   Lived in an alley;
Says the little boy to the little girl,
   " Shall I, oh! shall I? "

Says the little girl to the little boy,
   " What shall we do? "
Says the little boy to the little girl,
   " I will kiss you."

Three blind Mice.

THREE blind mice, see how they
      run!
They all ran after the farmer's wife,
Who cut off their tails with the carving-
    knife,
Did you ever see such a thing in your
    life?
            As three blind mice.

Curly Locks.

CURLY locks! curly locks! wilt thou
      be mine?
Thou shalt not wash dishes, nor yet feed
    the swine;
But sit on a cushion and sew a fine seam,
And feed upon strawberries, sugar, and
    cream!

Diddle, diddle Dumpling.

DIDDLE diddle dumpling, my son
      John,
Went to bed with his breeches on,
One stocking off, and one stocking on;
Diddle diddle dumpling, my son John.

A N old woman was sweeping her house, and she found a little crooked sixpence.

" What," said she, " shall I do with this little sixpence? I will go to market, and buy a little pig."

As she was coming home, she came to a stile; but the pig would not go over the stile.

She went a little farther, and she met a dog. So she said to the dog—

" Dog, dog, bite pig!
Pig won't get over the stile;
And I shan't get home to-night."

But the dog would not.

She went a little farther, and she met a stick. So she said—

" Stick, stick, beat dog!
Dog won't bite pig;
Pig won't get over the stile;
And I shan't get home to-night."

The old Woman and her Pig.

But the stick would not.

She went a little farther, and she met
a fire.   So she said—

> " Fire, fire, burn stick!
> Stick won't beat dog;
> Dog won't bite pig;
> Pig won't get over the stile;
> And I shan't get home to-night."

But the fire would not.

She went a little farther, and she met
some water.   So she said—

> "Water, water, quench fire!
> Fire won't burn stick;
> Stick won't beat dog;
> Dog won't bite pig;
> Pig won't get over the stile;
> And I shan't get home to-night."

But the water would not.

The old Woman and her Pig.

She went a little farther, and she met
an ox. So she said—

> "Ox, ox, drink water!
> Water won't quench fire;
> Fire won't burn stick;
> Stick won't beat dog;
> Dog won't bite pig;
> Pig won't get over the stile;
> And I shan't get home to-night."

But the ox would not.

She went a little farther, and she met
a butcher. So she said—

> "Butcher, butcher, kill ox!
> Ox won't drink water;
> Water won't quench fire;
> Fire won't burn stick;
> Stick won't beat dog;
> Dog won't bite pig;
> Pig won't get over the stile;
> And I shan't get home to-night."

But the butcher would not.

She went a little farther, and she met
a rope. So she said—

> "Rope, rope, hang butcher!
> Butcher won't kill ox;
> Ox won't drink water;
> Water won't quench fire;
> Fire won't burn stick;
> Stick won't beat dog;
> Dog won't bite pig;
> Pig won't get over the stile;
> And I shan't get home to-night."

But the rope would not.

She went a little farther, and she met
rat. So she said—

> "Rat, rat, gnaw rope!
> Rope won't hang butcher;
> Butcher won't kill ox;
> Ox won't drink water;

The old Woman and her Pig.

      Water won't quench fire;
      Fire won't burn stick;
      Stick won't beat dog;
      Dog won't bite pig;
      Pig won't get over the stile;
      And I shan't get home to-night."

But the rat would not.

She went a little farther, and she met
a cat. So she said—

      " Cat, cat, kill rat!
      Rat won't gnaw rope;
      Rope won't hang butcher;
      Butcher won't kill ox;
      Ox won't drink water;
      Water won't quench fire;
      Fire won't burn stick;
      Stick won't beat dog;
      Dog won't bite pig;
      Pig won't get over the stile;
      And I shan't get home to-night."

The old Woman and her Pig.

The cat said, "If you will give me a saucer of milk, I will kill the rat."

So the old woman gave the cat the milk, and when she had lapped up the milk—

The cat began to kill the rat;
The rat began to gnaw the rope;
The rope began to hang the butcher;
The butcher began to kill the ox;
The ox began to drink the water;
The water began to quench the fire;
The fire began to burn the stick;
The stick began to beat the dog;
The dog began to bite the pig;
The pig jumped over the stile;
And so the old woman got home that night.

Young Lambs to sell.

YOUNG Lambs to sell!
  Young Lambs to sell!
If I'd as much money as I can tell,
I never would cry—Young Lambs to sell!

86

Hey, my Kitten, my Kitten.

HEY, my kitten, my kitten,
And hey, my kitten, my deary!
Such a sweet pet as this
Was neither far nor neary.
Here we go up, up, up,
And here we go down, down, downy;
And here we go backwards and for-
wards,
And here we go round, round,
roundy.

Pussy sits beside the Fire.

PUSSY sits beside the fire,
How can she be fair?
In comes the little dog,
Pussy, are you there?
So, so, Mistress Pussy,
Pray how do you do?
Thank you, thank you, little dog,
I'm very well just now.

There was a Little Man
and he woo'd a Little Maid.

THERE was a little man,
  And he wooed a little maid,
And he said, "Little maid, will you wed,
    wed, wed?
  I have little more to say,
  Than will you, yea or nay,
For least said is soonest mended-ded,
    ded, ded."
  The little maid replied,
  Some say a little sighed,
"But what shall we have for to eat, eat,
    eat?
  Will the love that you're so rich in
  Make a fire in the kitchen?
Or the little god of Love turn the spit,
    spit, spit?"

Rain, Rain, go away.

RAIN, rain, go away;
  Come again another day;
  Little Susy wants to play.

High diddle ding.

HIGH diddle ding,
   Did you hear the bells ring?
The Parliament soldiers are gone to the
   King;
Some they did laugh, some they did cry,
To see the Parliament soldiers pass by.

One, two, three.

ONE, two, three,
I love coffee,
   And Billy loves tea.
How good you be,
One, two, three,
I love coffee,
   And Billy loves tea.

F FOR fig,
   J for jig,
And N for knuckle-bones,
J for John the waterman,
And S for sack of stones.

Blow, Wind, blow!
and go, Mill, go!

BLOW, wind, blow!
   and go, mill, go!
That the miller may
   grind his corn;
That the baker may take it,
And into rolls make it,
And send us some hot in
   the morn.

One, He loves.

ONE, he loves; two, he loves;
Three, he loves, they say;
Four, he loves with all his heart;
Five, he casts away.
Six, he loves; seven, she loves;
Eight, they both love.
Nine, he comes; ten, he tarries;
Eleven, he courts; twelve, he marries.

91

There once were two Cats.

THERE once were two cats of Kil-
kenny,
Each thought there was one cat too many,
So they fought and they fit,
And they scratched and they bit,
Till, excepting their nails
And the tips of their tails,
Instead of two cats, there weren't any.

The Cock's on the Housetop.

THE cock's on the housetop blowing
his horn;
The bull's in the barn a-threshing of corn;
The maids in the meadows are making of
hay,
The ducks in the river are swimming
away.

Two little Kittens.

TWO little kittens, one stormy night,
    Began to quarrel and then to fight;
One had a mouse, and the other had none,
And that's the way the quarrel begun.

"I'll have that mouse," said the biggest
    cat.
"*You'll* have that mouse? We'll see
    about that!"
"I *will* have that mouse," said the eldest
    son.
"You *shan't* have the mouse," said the
    little one.

I told you before 'twas a stormy night
When these two little kittens began to
    fight;
The old woman seized her sweeping
    broom,

Two little Kittens.

And swept the two kittens right out of
the room.

The ground was covered with frost and
snow,

And the two little kittens had nowhere to
go;

So they laid them down on the mat at the
door,

While the old woman finished sweeping
the floor.

Then they crept in, as quiet as mice,

All wet with the snow, and as cold as ice,

For they found it was better, that stormy
night,

To lie down and sleep than to quarrel and
fight.

Little Jack Horner.
Page 100

When I was a Bachelor.
Page 120

Humpty Dumpty.
Page 76

Twinkle, twinkle, little Star.
Page 110

Robin Hood.

ROBIN HOOD, Robin Hood,
 Is in the mickle wood!
Little John, Little John,
He to the town is gone.
Robin Hood, Robin Hood,
 Is telling his beads,
All in the greenwood,
 Among the green weeds.
Little John, Little John,
 If he comes no more,
Robin Hood, Robin Hood,
 We shall fret full sore!

What is the News of the Day?

WHAT is the news of the day,
 Good neighbour, I pray?
They say the balloon
Is gone up to the moon!

95

Come hither.

COME hither, little puppy dog;
   I'll give you a new collar,
If you will learn to read your book
   And be a clever scholar.
No, no! replied the puppy dog,
   I've other fish to fry,
For I must learn to guard your house,
   And bark when thieves come nigh.
With a tingle, tangle, tit-mouse!
   Robin knows great A,
And B, and C, and D, and E, F, G,
   H, I, J, K.

Come hither, pretty cockatoo;
   Come and learn your letters,
And you shall have a knife and fork
   To eat with, like your betters.
No, no! the cockatoo replied,
   My beak will do as well;
I'd rather eat my victuals thus
   Than go and learn to spell.

Come hither.

With a tingle, tangle, tit-mouse!
    Robin knows great A,
And B, and C, and D, and E, F, G,
    H, I, J, K.

Come hither, little pussy cat;
    If you'll your grammar study
I'll give you silver clogs to wear,
    Whene'er the gutter's muddy.
No! whilst I grammar learn, says Puss,
    Your house will in a trice
Be overrun from top to bottom
    With flocks of rats and mice.
With a tingle, tangle, tit-mouse!
    Robin knows great A,
And B, and C, and D, and E, F, G,
    H, I, J, K.

Come hither, then, good little boy,
    And learn your alphabet,
And you a pair of boots and spurs,
    Like your papa's, shall get.

Come hither.

Oh, yes! I'll learn my alphabet;
  And when I well can read,
Perhaps papa will give, me, too,
  A pretty long-tail'd steed.
With a tingle, tangle, tit-mouse!
  Robin knows great A,
And B, and C, and D, and E, F, G,
  H, I, J, K.

I had a little Hobby-horse.

I HAD a little hobby-horse,
  And it was dapple grey;
Its head was made of pea-straw,
  Its tail was made of hay.

I sold it to an old woman
  For a copper groat;
And I'll not sing my song again
  Without a new coat.

Two little Dogs.

TWO little dogs
Sat by the fire,
Over a fender of coal-dust;
Said one little dog
To the other little dog,
If you don't talk, why, I must.

Little Tom Twig.

LITTLE Tom Twig bought a fine
bow and arrow,
And what did he shoot? why, a poor little
sparrow.
Oh, fie, little Tom, with your fine bow and
arrow,
How cruel to shoot at a poor little sparrow.

One to make ready.

ONE to make ready,
And two to prepare;
Good luck to the rider,
And away goes the mare.

Ding, dong, bell.

DING, dong, bell,

The cat's in the well.

Who put her in?

Little Johnny Green.

Who pulled her out?

Great Johnny Stout.

What a naughty boy was that

To drown poor pussy cat,

Which never did him any harm,

But killed the mice in his father's barn.

Little Jack Horner.

LITTLE Jack Horner sat in a corner

Eating his Christmas pie.

He put in his thumb and pulled out a
plum

And said what a good boy am I.

Playmates.

PRAY, playmates agree.
E, F, and G,
Well, so it shall be.
J, K, and L,
In peace we will dwell.
M, N, and O,
To play let us go.
P, Q, R and S,
Love may we possess.
W, X, and Y,
Will not quarrel or die.
Z, and amperse—and,
Go to school at command.

Gunpowder Treason.

PLEASE to remember
The Fifth of November
Gunpowder treason and plot;
I know no reason
Why gunpowder treason
Should ever be forgot.

Kitty alone and I.

THERE was a frog lived in a well,
   Kitty alone, Kitty alone;
There was a frog lived in a well;
   Kitty alone and I!

There was a frog lived in a well;
And a farce* mouse in a mill,
Cock me carry, Kitty alone,
   Kitty alone and I.

This frog he would a-wooing ride,
   Kitty alone, &c.
This frog he would a-wooing ride,
And on a snail he got astride,
   Cock me carry, &c.

He rode till he came to my Lady Mouse
   Hall,
   Kitty alone, &c.
He rode till he came to my Lady Mouse
   Hall,
And there he did both knock and call,
   Cock me carry, &c.

* merry

Kitty alone and I.

Quoth he, "Miss Mouse, I'm come to
    thee,"—
  Kitty alone, &c.
Quoth he, "Miss Mouse, I'm come to
    thee,
To see if thou canst fancy me."
  Cock me carry, &c.

Quoth she, "Answer I'll give you
    none"—
  Kitty alone, &c.
Quoth she, "Answer I'll give you none
Until my Uncle Rat come home."
  Cock me carry, &c.

And when her Uncle Rat came home,
  Kitty alone, &c.
And when her Uncle Rat came home:
"Who's been here since I've been gone?"
  Cock me carry, &c.

"Sir, there's been a worthy gentleman"—
  Kitty alone, &c.

Kitty alone and I.

" Sir, there's been a worthy gentleman—
That's been here since you've been
    gone."
    Cock me carry, &c.

The frog he came whistling through the
    brook,
    Kitty alone, &c.
The frog he came whistling through the
    brook,
And there he met with a dainty duck.
    Cock me carry, &c.

This duck she swallowed him up with a
    pluck,
    Kitty alone, Kitty alone;
This duck she swallowed him up with a
    pluck,
So there's an end of my history-book.
    Cock me carry, Kitty alone,
    Kitty alone and I.

Para-mara, dictum, domine.

I HAVE four sisters beyond the sea,
  Para-mara, dictum, domine.
And they did send four presents to me,
  Partum, quartum, paradise, tempum,
  Para-mara, dictum, domine!

The first it was a bird without e'er a bone;
  Para-mara, dictum, &c.
The second was a cherry without e'er a
    stone;
  Para-mara, dictum, &c.

The third it was a blanket without e'er a
    thread,
  Para-mara, dictum, &c.
The fourth it was a book which no man
    could read;
  Partum, quartum, &c.

How can there be a bird without e'er a
    bone?
  Para-mara, dictum, &c.

Para-mara, dictum, domine.

How can there be a cherry without e'er a
    stone?
Partum, quartum, &c.

How can there be a blanket without e'er
    a thread?
Para-mara, dictum, &c.
How can there be a book which no man
    can read?
Partum, quartum, &c.

When the bird's in the shell, there is no
    bone;
Para-mara, dictum, &c.
When the cherry's in the bud, there is no
    stone;
Partum, quartum, &c.

When the blanket's in the fleece, there is
    no thread;
Para-mara, dictum, &c.
When the book's in the press, no man can
    read;
Partum, quartum, &c.

There was an old Woman.

THERE was an old woman who lived
    in a shoe,
She had so many children she didn't know
    what to do;
She gave them some broth without any
    bread,
She whipped them all round, and sent
    them to bed.

Polly, put the Kettle on.

POLLY, put the kettle on,
Polly, put the kettle on,
Polly, put the kettle on,
    And we'll all have tea.

Sukey, take it off again,
Sukey, take it off again,
Sukey, take it off again,
    They're all gone away.

Doctor Foster.

DOCTOR FOSTER went to Glo'ster,
    In a shower of rain;
He stepped in a puddle, up to his middle,
And never went there again.

Tommy Snooks and Betsey Brooks.

AS Tommy Snooks and Betsey
     Brooks
Were walking out one Sunday,
Said Tommy Snooks to Betsey Brooks,
To-morrow will be Monday.

There was a Man of our Town.

THERE was a man of our town,
     And he was wondrous wise,
He jump'd into a bramble bush,
     And scratch'd out both his eyes:
But when he saw his eyes were out,
     With all his might and main
He jump'd into another hedge,
     And scratch'd 'em in again.

The King of France.

THE King of France went up the hill,
     With twenty thousand men;
The King of France came down the hill,
     And ne'er went up again.

Tommy Snooks and Betsey Brooks.

Twinkle, twinkle, little Star.

TWINKLE, twinkle, little star,
How I wonder what you are,
Up above the world so high,
Like a diamond in the sky.

When the blazing sun is gone,
When he nothing shines upon,
Then you show your little light,
Twinkle, twinkle, all the night.

Then the traveller in the dark
Thanks you for your tiny spark;
How could he see where to go,
If you did not twinkle so?

In the dark blue sky you keep,
Often through my curtains peep,
For you never shut your eye,
Till the sun is in the sky.

As your bright and tiny spark
Lights the traveller in the dark,
Though I know not what you are,
Twinkle, twinkle, little star.

The Alphabet.

A was an angler,
  Went out in a fog;
Who fish'd all the day,
  And caught only a frog.

B was cook Betty,
  A-baking a pie
With ten or twelve apples
  All piled up on high.

C was a custard
  In a glass dish,
With as much cinnamon
  As you could wish.

D was fat Dick,
  Who did nothing but eat;
He would leave book and play
  For a nice bit of meat.

E was an egg,
  In a basket with more,
Which Peggy will sell
  For a shilling a score.

The Alphabet.

F was a fox,
  So cunning and sly:
Who looks at the hen-roost—
  I need not say why.

G was a greyhound,
  As fleet as the wind;
In the race or the course
  Left all others behind.

H was a heron,
  Who lived near a pond;
Of gobbling the fishes
  He was wondrously fond.

I was the ice
  On which Billy would skate;
So up went his heels,
  And down went his pate.

J was Joe Jenkins,
  Who played on the fiddle;
He began twenty tunes,
  But left off in the middle.

112

The Alphabet.

K was a kitten,
    Who jumped at a cork,
And learned to eat mice
    Without plate, knife, or fork.

L was a lark,
    Who sings us a song,
And wakes us betimes
    Lest we sleep too long.

M was Miss Molly,
    Who turned in her toes,
And hung down her head
    Till her knees touched her nose.

N was a nosegay,
    Sprinkled with dew,
Pulled in the morning
    And presented to you.

O was an owl,
    Who looked wondrously wise;
But he's watching a mouse
    With his large round eyes.

The Alphabet.

P was a parrot,
>With feathers like gold,
Who talks just as much,
>And no more than he's told.

Q is the Queen
>Who governs the land,
And sits on a throne
>Very lofty and grand.

R is a raven
>Perched on an oak,
Who with a gruff voice
>Cries croak, croak, croak!

S was a stork
>With a very long bill,
Who swallows down fishes
>And frogs to his fill.

T is a trumpeter
>Blowing his horn,
Who tells us the news
>As we rise in the morn.

The Alphabet.

U is a unicorn,
    Who, as it is said,
  Wears an ivory bodkin
    On his forehead.

V is a vulture
    Who eats a great deal,
  Devouring a dog
    Or a cat as a meal.

W was a watchman
    Who guarded the street,
  Lest robbers or thieves
    The good people should meet.

X was King Xerxes,
    Who, if you don't know,
  Reigned over Persia
    A great while ago.

Y is the year
    That is passing away,
  And still growing shorter
    Every day.

The Alphabet.

Z is a zebra,
> Whom you've heard of before;
So here ends my rhyme
> Till I find you some more.

Billy Pringle's Pig.

HAVE you ever heard of Billy Prin-
> gle's pig?
It was very little and not very big;
When it was alive it lived in clover;
But now it's dead, and that's all over.
Billy Pringle he lay down and died,
Betsy Pringle she sat down and cried;
So there's an end of all the three,
Billy Pringle he, Betsy Pringle she, and
> poor little piggy wigee.

Hey, dorolot!

HEY, dorolot, dorolot!
> Hey, dorolay, dorolay!
Hey, my bonny boat, bonny boat,
> Hey, drag away, drag away!

Three little Kittens.

THREE little kittens lost their mit-
tens,
And they began to cry,
Oh! mother dear,
We very much fear
That we have lost our mittens.

Lost your mittens!
You naughty kittens!
Then you shall have no pie.
Mee-ow, mee-ow, mee-ow.
No, you shall have no pie.
Mee-ow, mee-ow, mee-ow.

The three little kittens found their mit-
tens,
And they began to cry,
Oh! mother dear,
See here, see here!
See, we have found our mittens.

Three little Kittens.

Put on your mittens,
You silly kittens,
And you shall have some pie,
Purr-r, purr-r, purr-r,
Oh! let us have the pie!
Purr-r, purr-r, purr-r,

The three little kittens put on their mit-
tens,
And soon ate up the pie;
Oh! mother dear,
We greatly fear,
That we have soiled our mittens.

Soiled your mittens!
You naughty kittens!
Then they began to sigh,
Mi-ow, mi-ow, mi-ow.
Then they began to sigh,
Mi-ow, mi-ow, mi-ow.

Three little Kittens.

The three little kittens washed their mit-
tens,
And hung them up to dry;
Oh! mother dear,
Do you not hear,
That we have washed our mittens?

Washed your mittens!
Oh! you're good kittens.
But I smell a rat close by.
Hush! hush! mee-ow, mee-ow.
We smell a rat close by,
Mee-ow, mee-ow, mee-ow.

Peter Piper

PETER PIPER picked a peck of
pickled pepper;
A peck of pickled pepper Peter Piper
picked;
If Peter Piper picked a peck of pickled
pepper,
Where's the peck of pickled pepper Peter
Piper picked?

When I was a Bachelor.

WHEN I was a bachelor I lived by
    myself,
And all the meat I got I put upon a shelf,
The rats and the mice did lead me such
    a life,
That I went to London, to get myself a
    wife.

The streets were so broad, and the lanes
    were so narrow,
I could not get my wife home without a
    wheelbarrow,
The wheelbarrow broke, my wife got a
    fall,
Down tumbled wheelbarrow, little wife,
    and all.

Jocky was a Piper's Son.

JOCKY was a piper's son,
    And he fell in love when he
    was young,
And the only tune that he could play
Was, "Over the hills and far away";
Over the hills and a great way off,
And the wind will blow my top-knot off.

120

One, two, buckle my Shoe.

ONE, two,
Buckle my shoe;
Three, four,
Shut the door;
Five, six,
Pick up sticks;
Seven, eight,
Lay them straight;
Nine, ten,
A good fat hen;
Eleven, twelve,
Who will delve?
Thirteen, fourteen,
Maids a-courting;
Fifteen, sixteen,
Maids in the kitchen;
Seventeen, eighteen,
Maids a-waiting;
Nineteen, twenty,
My plate's empty.

A carrion Crow.

A CARRION crow sat on an oak,
   Fol de riddle, lol de riddle, hi ding
     do,
Watching a tailor shape his coat;
   Sing heigh ho, the carrion crow,
   Fol de riddle, lol de riddle, hi ding do.

Monday's Bairn.

MONDAY'S bairn is fair of face,
   Tuesday's bairn is full of grace,
Wednesday's bairn is full of woe,
Thursday's bairn has far to go,
Friday's bairn is loving and giving,
Saturday's bairn works hard for its living,
But the bairn that is born on the Sabbath
   day
Is bonny and blythe and good and gay.

January brings the Snow.

J ANUARY brings the snow,
Makes our feet and fingers glow.

February brings the rain,
Thaws the frozen lake again.

March brings breezes loud and shrill,
Stirs the dancing daffodil.

April brings the primrose sweet,
Scatters daisies at our feet.

May brings flocks of pretty lambs,
Skipping by their fleecy dams.

June brings tulips, lilies, roses,
Fills the children's hands with posies.

Hot July brings cooling showers,
Apricots and gillyflowers.

January brings the Snow.

August brings the sheaves of corn,
Then the harvest home is borne.

Warm September brings the fruit,
Sportsmen then begin to shoot.

Fresh October brings the pheasant,
Then to gather nuts is pleasant.

Dull November brings the blast,
Then the leaves are whirling fast.

Chill December brings the sleet,
Blazing fire and Christmas treat.

Bless you, Burny-Bee.

BLESS you, bless you, burny-bee:
Say, when will your wedding be?
If it be to-morrow day,
Take your wings and fly away.

Simple Simon met a Pieman.
Page 140

Little Miss Muffet.
Page 160

The House that Jack built.
Page 125

The House that Jack built.
Page 125

The House that Jack built.

THIS is the house that Jack built.
This is the malt
That lay in the house that Jack built.

This is the rat,
That ate the malt
That lay in the house that Jack built.

This is the cat,
That killed the rat,
That ate the malt
That lay in the house that Jack built.

This is the dog,
That worried the cat,
That killed the rat,
That ate the malt
That lay in the house that Jack built.

This is the cow with the crumpled horn,
That tossed the dog,
That worried the cat,
That killed the rat,
That ate the malt

The House that Jack built.

That lay in the house that Jack built.

This is the maiden all forlorn,
That milked the cow with the crumpled
    horn,
That tossed the dog,
That worried the cat,
That killed the rat,
That ate the malt
That lay in the house that Jack built.

This is the man all tattered and torn,
That kissed the maiden all forlorn,
That milked the cow with the crumpled
    horn,
That tossed the dog,
That worried the cat,
That killed the rat,
That ate the malt
That lay in the house that Jack built.

This is the priest all shaven and shorn,

The House that Jack built.
Page 126

The House that Jack built.
Page 126

The House that Jack built.

That married the man all tattered and
    torn,
That kissed the maiden all forlorn,
That milked the cow with the crumpled
    horn,
That tossed the dog,
That worried the cat,
That killed the rat,
That ate the malt
That lay in the house that Jack built.

This is the cock that crowed in the morn,
That waked the priest all shaven and
    shorn,
That married the man all tattered and
    torn,
That kissed the maiden all forlorn,
That milked the cow with the crumpled
    horn,
That tossed the dog,
That worried the cat,
That killed the rat,

The House that Jack built.

That ate the malt
That lay in the house that Jack built.

This is the farmer sowing his corn,
That kept the cock that crowed in the
morn,
That waked the priest all shaven and
shorn,
That married the man all tattered and
torn,
That kissed the maiden all forlorn,
That milked the cow with the crumpled
horn,
That tossed the dog,
That worried the cat,
That killed the rat,
That ate the malt
That lay in the house that Jack built.

THE calf, the goose, the bee,
The world is ruled by these three.
(Parchment, pens, and wax.)

When I was a little Girl.

WHEN I was a little girl, about seven
years old,
I hadn't got a petticoat to cover me from
the cold;
So I went into Darlington, that pretty
little town,
And there I bought a petticoat, a cloak,
and a gown,
I went into the woods and built me a
kirk,
And all the birds of the air, they helped
me to work.
The hawk, with his long claws, pulled
down the stone,
The dove, with her rough bill, brought
me them home:
The parrot was the clergyman, the pea-
cock was the clerk,
The bullfinch played the organ, and we
made merry work.

Ring around a Rosie.

RING around a rosie,
A bottle full of posie,
All the girls in our town,
Ring for little Josie.

*When good King Arthur
ruled this Land.*

WHEN good King Arthur ruled
this land,
  He was a goodly king;
He stole three pecks of barley-meal,
  To make a bag-pudding.

A bag-pudding the king did make,
  And stuff'd it well with plums:
And in it put great lumps of fat,
  As big as my two thumbs.

The king and queen did eat thereof,
  And noblemen beside;
And what they could not eat that night,
  The queen next morning fried.

Needles and Pins.

NEEDLES and pins, needles and
pins,
When a man marries his trouble begins.

Old Grimes.

OLD Grimes is dead, that good old
man,
You'll never see him more;
He used to wear a long brown coat,
That buttoned down before.

The fat Man of Bombay.

THERE was a fat man of Bombay,
Who was smoking one sunshiny
day,
When a bird, called a snipe,
Flew away with his pipe,
Which vexed the fat man of Bombay.

What Shoemaker?

WHAT shoemaker makes shoes with-
out leather,
With all the four elements put together?
Fire and water, earth and air;
Every customer has two pair.

(*A horse-shoer.*)

132

Little blue Betty.

LITTLE Blue Betty lived in a lane,
She sold good ale to gentlemen:
Gentlemen came every day,
And little Betty Blue hopped away.
She hopped upstairs to make her bed,
And she tumbled down and broke her head.

A Riddle.

THERE was a little green house
And in the little green house
There was a little brown house,
And in the little brown house
There was a little yellow house,
And in the little yellow house
There was a little white house,
And in the little white house
There was a little heart.

(*A walnut.*)

Oh, deary, deary me.

THERE was an old woman, as I've
heard tell,
She went to market her eggs for to sell;
She went to market all on a market day,
And she fell asleep on the King's high-
way.

There came by a pedlar, whose name was
Stout,—
He cut her petticoats all round about;
He cut her petticoats up to the knees,
Which made the old woman to shiver and
freeze.

When this little woman first did wake,
She began to shiver and she began to
shake,
She began to wonder and she began to
cry,
"Oh! deary, deary me, this is none of I!

Oh, deary, deary me.

"But if it be I, as I do hope it be,
I have a little dog at home, and he'll know
  me;
If it be I, he'll wag his little tail,
And if it be not I, he'll loudly bark and
  wail."

Home went the little woman all in the
  dark;
Up got the little dog, and he began to
  bark;
He began to bark, so she began to cry,
"Oh! deary, deary me, this is none of I!"

IN fir tar is,
In oak none is.
In mud eel is,
In clay none is.
Goat eat ivy,
Mare eat oats.

Bobby Shaftoe.

BOBBY SHAFTOE'S gone to sea,
Silver buckles on his knee;
He'll come back and marry me,
Bonny Bobby Shaftoe!
Bobby Shaftoe's young and fair,
Combing down his yellow hair,
He's my love for evermore,
Bonny Bobby Shaftoe.

As I was going up Pippen Hill.

AS I was going up Pippen Hill,
Pippen Hill was dirty;
There I met a pretty miss,
And she dropped me a curtsey.

Little miss, pretty miss,
Blessings light upon you!
If I had half-a-crown a day,
I'd spend it all on you.

Cock a doodle doo!

COCK a doodle doo!
My dame has lost her shoe;
My master's lost his fiddling stick,
And don't know what to do.

Cock a doodle doo!
What is my dame to do?
Till master finds his fiddling stick,
She'll dance without her shoe.

Cock a doodle doo!
My dame has lost her shoe,
And master's found his fiddling stick,
Sing doodle doodle doo!

Cock a doodle doo!
My dame will dance with you.
While master fiddles his fiddling stick,
For dame and doodle doo.

Cock a doodle doo!
Dame has lost her shoe;
Gone to bed and scratched her head,
And can't tell what to do.

Little Willie Winkle.

LITTLE Willie Winkle runs through
   the town,
Upstairs and downstairs, in his nightgown,
Rapping at the window, crying through
   the lock,
"Are the children in their beds? for now
   it's eight o'clock."

Little King Boggen.

LITTLE King Boggen he built a
   fine hall,
Pie-crust and pastry-crust, that was the
   wall;
The windows were made of black-pud-
   dings and white,
And slated with pancakes;—you ne'er
   saw the like.

The Queen of Hearts.

THE Queen of Hearts,
She made some tarts,
   All on a summer's day;

The Knave of Hearts,
He stole those tarts,
   And took them clean away.

The King of Hearts
Called for the tarts,
   And beat the Knave full sore;

The Knave of Hearts
Brought back the tarts,
   And vowed he'd steal no more.

Yankee Doodle.

YANKEE DOODLE went to
   town,
   Upon a little pony;
He stuck a feather in his hat,
   And called it Macaroni.

Simple Simon met a Pieman.

SIMPLE SIMON met a pieman
    Going to the fair;
Says Simple Simon to the pieman,
    "Let me taste your ware."

Says the pieman to Simple Simon,
    " Show me first your penny."
Says Simple Simon to the pieman,
    "Indeed, I have not any."

Simple Simon went a-fishing,
    For to catch a whale:
All the water he had got
    Was in his mother's pail.

Here's Sulky Sue.

HERE'S Sulky Sue,
What shall we do?
    Turn her face to the wall
    Till she comes to.

The Queen of Hearts.
Page 139

Simple Simon met a Pieman.
Page 140

This is the way the Ladies ride.

THIS is the way the ladies ride;
    Tri, tre, tre, tree,
    Tri, tre, tre, tree!
This is the way the ladies ride,
    Tri tre, tre, tre, tri-tre-tre-tree!

This is the way the gentlemen ride;
    Gallop-a-trot,
    Gallop-a-trot!
This is the way the gentlemen ride;
    Gallop-a-gallop-a-trot!

This is the way the farmers ride;
    Hobbledy-hoy,
    Hobbledy-hoy!
This is the way the farmers ride,
    Hobbledy hobbledy-hoy!

Early to Bed.

EARLY to bed, and early to rise,
Makes a man healthy, wealthy,
    and wise.

141

The Days of the Month.

THIRTY days hath September,
April, June and November;
February has twenty-eight alone,
All the rest have thirty-one,
Excepting leap-year, that's the
  time
When February's days are twenty-
  nine.

Little Tommy Tittlemouse.

LITTLE Tommy Tittlemouse
Lived in a little house;
He caught fishes
In other men's ditches.

Little Tee Wee.

LITTLE Tee Wee,
He went to sea
In an open boat;
And while afloat
The little boat bended,
And my story's ended.

The Spider and the Fly.

"WILL you walk into my parlour?"
    said the spider to the fly,—
" 'Tis the prettiest little parlour that ever
    you did spy.
The way into my parlour is up a winding
    stair;
And I have many curious things to show
    you when you're there."
"Oh no, no," said the little fly; "to ask
    me is in vain;
For who goes up your winding stair can
    ne'er come down again."
"I'm sure you must be weary, dear, with
    soaring up so high;
Will you rest upon my little bed?" said
    the spider to the fly.
"There are pretty curtains drawn
    around; the sheets are fine and thin;
And if you like to rest awhile, I'll snugly
    tuck you in!"
"Oh no, no," said the little fly; "for I've
    often heard it said,
They never, never wake again who sleep
    upon your bed!"

The Spider and the Fly.

Said the cunning spider to the fly—
 "Dear friend, what can I do
To prove the warm affection I've always
    felt for you?
I have within my pantry good store of
    all that's nice;
I'm sure you're very welcome—will you
    please to take a slice?"
"Oh no, no," said the little fly, "kind sir,
    that cannot be;
I've heard what's in your pantry and I
    do not wish to see."

"Sweet creature," said the spider, "you're
    witty and you're wise;
How handsome are your gauzy wings,
    how brilliant are your eyes!
I have a little looking-glass upon my
    parlour shelf,
If you'll step in one moment, dear, you
    shall behold yourself."
"I thank you, gentle sir," she said, "for
    what you're pleased to say,
And bidding you good-morning now, I'll
    call another day."

The Spider and the Fly.

The spider turned him round about, and
 went into his den,
For well he knew the silly fly would soon
 come back again;
So he wove a subtle web in a little corner
 sly,
And set his table ready, to dine upon the
 fly.
Then he came out to his door again, and
 merrily did sing,—
"Come hither, hither, pretty fly, with the
 pearl and silver wing;
Your robes are green and purple—there's
 a crest upon your head!
Your eyes are like the diamond bright, but
 mine are dull as lead!"

Alas! alas! how very soon this silly little
 fly,
Hearing his wily, flattering words, came
 slowly flitting by.
With buzzing wings she hung aloft, then
 near and nearer drew,

The Spider and the Fly.

Thinking only of her brilliant eyes, her
  green and purple hue—
Thinking only of her crested head—poor
  foolish thing! At last,
Up jumped the cunning spider, and
  fiercely held her fast!
He dragged her up his winding stair,
  into his dismal den,
Within his little parlour—but she ne'er
  came out again!

And now, dear little children, who may
  this story read,
To idle, silly flattering words, I pray you,
  ne'er give heed;
Unto an evil counsellor close heart, and
  ear, and eye,
And take a lesson from this tale of the
  Spider and the Fly.

146

Lock and Key.

I AM a gold lock.

I am a gold key.

I am a silver lock.

I am a silver key.

I am a brass lock.

I am a brass key.

I am a lead lock.

I am a lead key.

I am a monk lock.

I am a monk key!

St. Swithin's Day.

ST. SWITHIN'S DAY, if thou dost rain,
For forty days it will remain:
St. Swithin's Day, if thou be fair,
For forty days 'twill rain na mair.

147

Billy, Billy, come and play.

BILLY, Billy, come and play,
While the sun shines bright as day."

" Yes, my Polly, so I will,
For I love to please you still."

" Billy, Billy, have you seen,
Sam and Betsy on the green? "

" Yes, my Poll, I saw them pass,
Skipping o'er the new-mown grass."

" Billy, Billy, come along,
And I will sing a pretty song."

" O then, Polly, I'll make haste,
Not one moment will I waste,
But will come and hear you sing,
And my fiddle I will bring."

London Bridge is falling down.

LONDON Bridge is falling down,
  Falling down, falling down;
London Bridge is falling down,
  My fair lady.

You've stole my watch and kept my keys,
Kept my keys, kept my keys;
You've stole my watch and kept my keys,
  My fair lady.

Off to prison she must go,
She must go, she must go;
Off to prison she must go,
  My fair lady.

Take the key and lock her up,
Lock her up, lock her up;
Take the key and lock her up,
  My fair lady.

Elsie Marley.

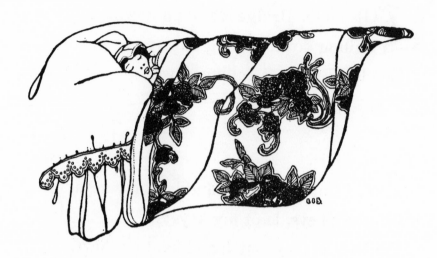

ELSIE MARLEY is grown so fine,
She won't get up to serve the swine,
But lies in bed till eight or nine,
And surely she does take her time.

And do you ken Elsie Marley, honey?
The wife who sells the barley, honey;
She won't get up to serve her swine,
And do you ken Elsie Marley, honey?

Jack and Jill.
Page 180

Mary, Mary, quite contrary.
Page 200

A little cock Sparrow.

A LITTLE cock sparrow sat on a green tree.
And he cherupped, he cherupped, so merry was he.
A little cock sparrow sat on a green tree,
And he cherupped, he cherupped, so merry was he.

A naughty boy came with his wee bow and arrow,
Determined to shoot this little cock sparrow,
A naughty boy came with his wee bow and arrow,
Determined to shoot this little cock sparrow.

"This little cock sparrow shall make me a stew,
And his giblets shall make me a little pie too."
"Oh, no!" said the sparrow, "I *won't* make a stew."
So he flapped his wings and away he flew!

There was an old Woman.

THERE was an old woman who rode
  on a broom,
 With a high gee ho, gee humble;
And she took her old cat behind for a
  groom,
 With a bimble, bamble, bumble.

They travelled along till they came to the
  sky,
 With a high gee ho, gee humble;
But the journey so long made them very
  hungry,
 With a bimble, bamble, bumble.

Says Tom, "I can find nothing here to
  eat,
 With a high gee ho, gee humble;
So let us go back again, I entreat,
 With a bimble, bamble, bumble."

The old woman would not go back so
　　soon,
　　With a high gee ho, gee humble;
For she wanted to visit the Man in the
　　Moon,
　　With a bimble, bamble, bumble.

Says Tom, "I'll go back by myself to our
　　house,
　　With a high gee ho, gee humble;
For there I can catch a good rat or a
　　mouse,
　　With a bimble, bamble, bumble."

"But," says the old woman, "how will
　　you go?
　　With a high gee ho, gee humble;
You shan't have my nag, I protest and
　　vow,
　　With a bimble, bamble, bumble."

"No, no," says Tom, "I've a plan of my
　　own,

There was an old Woman.

With a high gee ho, gee humble; "
So he slid down the rainbow, and left her
  alone,
With a bimble, bamble, bumble.

So now, if you happen to visit the sky,
  With a high gee ho, gee humble,
And want to come back, you Tom's
  method may try,
With a bimble, bamble, bumble.

If Wishes were Horses.

IF wishes were horses,
  Beggars would ride;
  If turnips were watches,
  I would wear one by my side.

FORMED long ago, yet made to-day,
  Employed while others sleep;
What few would like to give away,
  Nor any wish to keep.

(*A bed.*)

A FROG he would a-wooing go,
        Heigho, says Rowley,
Whether his mother would let him or no,
    With a rowley powley, gammon and
      spinach,
    Heigho, says Anthony Rowley!

So off he set with his opera hat,
        Heigho, says Rowley,
And on the road he met with a rat.
    With a rowley powley, gammon and
      spinach,
    Heigho, says Anthony Rowley!

"Pray, Mr. Rat, will you go with me,"
        Heigho, says Rowley,
" Kind Mrs. Mousey for to see?"
    With a rowley powley, gammon and
      spinach,
    Heigho, says Anthony Rowley!

A Frog he would a-wooing go.

When they reached the door of Mousey's
hall,

Heigho, says Rowley,

They gave a loud knock, and they gave a
loud call.

With a rowley powley, gammon and
spinach,

Heigho, says Anthony Rowley!

"Pray, Mrs. Mouse, are you within?"

Heigho, says Rowley,

"Oh, yes, kind sirs, I'm sitting to spin."

With a rowley powley, gammon and
spinach,

Heigho, says Anthony Rowley!

"Pray, Mrs. Mouse, will you gve us some
beer?

Heigho, says Rowley,

For Froggy and I are fond of good
cheer."

With a rowley powley, gammon and
spinach,

Heigho, says Anthony Rowley!

A Frog he would a-wooing go.

"Pray, Mr. Frog, will you give us a song?
         Heigho, says Rowley.
But let it be something that's not very
    long."
    With a rowley powley, gammon and
        spinach,
    Heigho, says Anthony Rowley!

" Indeed, Mrs. Mouse," replied Mr. Frog,
         Heigho, says Rowley,
" A cold has made me as hoarse as a hog."
    With a rowley powley, gammon and
        spinach,
    Heigho, says Anthony Rowley!

" Since you have caught cold, Mr. Frog,"
    Mousey said,
         Heigho, says Rowley,
" I'll sing you a song that I have just
    made."
    With a rowley powley, gammon and
        spinach,
    Heigho, says Anthony Rowley!

157

A Frog he would a-wooing go.

But while they were all a merry-making,
> Heigho, says Rowley,
A cat and her kittens came tumbling in.
> With a rowley powley, gammon and
> spinach,
> Heigho, says Anthony Rowley!

The cat she seized the rat by the crown;
> Heigho, says Rowley,
The kittens they pulled the little mouse
down.
> With a rowley powley, gammon and
> spinach,
> Heigho, says Anthony Rowley!

This put Mr. Frog in a terrible fright;
> Heigho, says Rowley,
He took up his hat, and he wished them
good-night.
> With a rowley powley, gammon and
> spinach,
> Heigho, says Anthony Rowley!

A Frog he would a-wooing go.

But as Froggy was crossing over a brook,
　　　　　Heigho, says Rowley,
A lily-white duck came and gobbled him
　　up.
　　With a rowley powley, gammon and
　　　spinach,
　　Heigho, says Anthony Rowley!

So there was an end of one, two, and
　　three,
　　　　　Heigho, says Rowley,
The Rat, the Mouse, and the little Frog-
　　gee!
　　With a rowley powley, gammon and
　　　spinach,
　　Heigho, says Anthony Rowley!

I do not like thee, Doctor Fell.

I DO not like thee, Doctor Fell,
　The reason why I cannot tell;
But this I know, and know full well,
I do not like thee, Doctor Fell.

Little Miss Muffet.

LITTLE Miss Muffet sat on a tuf-
   fet,
Eating of curds and whey;
Along came a spider and sat down beside
   her,
And frightened Miss Muffet away.

The Rose is red.

THE rose is red, the violet blue;
   Sugar is sweet—and so are you.
These are the words you bade me say
For a pair of new gloves on Easter day.

Baa, baa, black Sheep.

BAA, baa, black sheep, have you any
   wool?
Yes, sir, yes, sir, three bags full:
One for the master, one for the dame,
And one for the little boy who lives in
   the lane.

A Frog he would a-wooing go.
Page 155

Sing a Song of Sixpence.
Page 170

As I was going to sell my Eggs.

AS I was going to sell my eggs
 I met a man with bandy legs;
Bandy legs and crooked toes,
I tripped up his heels, and he fell on his
 nose.

Willy Boy, where are you going?

WILLY boy, Willy boy, where are you
 going?
 I will go with you, if that I may.
I'm going to the meadow to see them a
 mowing,
 I'm going to help them make the hay.

Now what do you think?

NOW what do you think
 Of little Jack Jingle?
 Before he was married
 He used to live single.

With a Hop, Step,
and a Jump.

THE miller he grinds his corn, his
corn;

The miller he grinds his corn, his corn;

The little boy blue comes winding his

horn,

    With a hop, step, and a jump.

The carter he whistles aside his team;

The carter he whistles aside his team;

And Dolly comes tripping with the nice

clouted cream,

    With a hop, step, and a jump.

The nightingale sings when we're at rest;

The nightingale sings when we're at rest;

The little bird climbs the tree for his nest,

    With a hop, step, and a jump.

With a Hop, Step,
and a Jump.

The damsels are churning for curds and
whey;
The damsels are churning for curds and
whey;
The lads in the field are making the hay,
With a hop, step, and a jump.

He loves me.

1. He loves me,
2.   He don't!
3. He'll have me,
4.   He won't!
5. He would if he could,
6. But he can't,
7.   So he don't!

SPEAK when you're spoken to,
Come when one call,
Shut the door after you,
And turn to the wall.

Come, my Children.

COME, my children, come away,
  For the sun shines bright to-day;
Little children, come with me,
Birds and brooks and posies see;
Get your hats and come away,
For it is a pleasant day.

Everything is laughing, singing,
All the pretty flowers are springing;
See the kitten, full of fun,
Sporting in the brilliant sun;
Children too may sport and play,
For it is a pleasant day.

AWAKE, arise, pull out your eyes,
  And hear what time of day;
And when you have done, pull out your
  tongue,
And see what you can say.

The way we ride.

To market ride the gentlemen,
    So do we, so do we;
Then comes the country clowns,
    Hobbledy gee, Hobbledy gee;
First go the ladies, nim, nim, nim;
Next come the gentlemen, trim, trim,
    trim;
Then come the country clowns, gallop-a-
    trot.

One-ery, two-ery.

One-ery, two-ery,
Ziccary zan;
    Hollow bone, crack a bone,
    Ninery, ten;
    Spittery spot,
    It must be done;
    Twiddleum twaddleum,
    Twenty-one.

Now we dance looby, looby, looby.

NOW we dance looby, looby, looby,
  Now we dance looby, looby, light.
Shake your right hand a little,
And turn you round about.

Now we dance looby, looby, looby,
Shake your right hand a little,
Shake your left hand a little,
And turn you round about.

Now we dance looby, looby, looby,
Shake your right hand a little,
Shake your left hand a little,
Shake your right foot a little,
And turn you round about.

Now we dance looby, looby, looby,
Shake your right hand a little,
Shake your left hand a little,
Shake your right foot a little,
Shake your left foot a little,
And turn you round about.

166

Now we dance looby, looby, looby.

Now we dance looby, looby, looby,
Shake your right hand a little,
Shake your left hand a little,
Shake your right foot a little,
Shake your left foot a little,
Shake your head a little,
And turn you round about.

I'll sing you a Song.

I'LL sing you a song,
Though not very long,
Yet I think it as pretty as any;
Put your hand in your purse,
You'll never be worse,
And give the poor singer a penny.

HERE goes my lord
A trot, a trot, a trot, a trot!
Here goes my lady
A canter, a canter, a canter, a canter!

167

Round the Bramble Bush.

HERE we go round the bramble-bush,
  The bramble-bush. the bramble-
    bush;
Here we go round the bramble-bush
  On a cold frosty morning!

This is the way we wash our clothes,
  Wash our clothes, wash our clothes;
This is the way we wash our clothes
  On a cold frosty morning!

This is the way we clean our rooms,
  Clean our rooms, clean our rooms;
This is the way we clean our rooms
  On a cold frosty morning!

Here we go round the mulberry-bush,
  The mulberry-bush, the mulberry-
    bush;
Here we go round the mulberry-bush
  On a sunshiny morning.

Little Bo-Peep.

LITTLE Bo-Peep has lost her sheep,
    And can't tell where to find them;
Leave them alone, and they'll come home,
Wagging their tails behind them.

Little Bo-Peep.

Little Bo-Peep fell fast asleep,
And dreamt she heard them bleating;
When she awoke, 'twas a joke—
Ah! cruel vision so fleeting.

Then up she took her little crook,
Determined for to find them;
What was her joy to behold them nigh,
Wagging their tails behind them.

Sing a Song of Sixpence.

SING a song of sixpence,
Pocket full of rye;
Four and twenty blackbirds
Baked in a pie.

When the pie was opened
The birds began to sing—
Oh, wasn't that a dainty dish
To set before the king?

There was a Man,
and he was mad.

THERE was a man and he was mad,
 And he jumped into a pea-swad;
The pea-swad was over-full,
So he jumped into a roaring bull;
The roaring bull was over-fat,
So he jumped into a gentleman's hat;
The gentleman's hat was over-fine,
So he jumped into a bottle of wine;
The bottle of wine was over-dear,
So he jumped into a barrel of beer;
The barrel of beer was over-thick,
So he jumped into a club-stick;
The club-stick was over-narrow,
So he jumped into a wheelbarrow;
The wheelbarrow began to crack,
So he jumped on to a hay-stack;
The hay-stack began to blaze,
So he did nothing but cough and sneeze!

Christmas days.

THE first day of Christmas,
My true love sent to me
A partridge in a pear-tree.

The second day of Christmas,
My true love sent to me
Two turtle-doves, and
A partridge in a pear-tree.

The third day of Christmas,
My true love sent to me
Three French hens,
Two turtle-doves, and
A partridge in a pear-tree.

The fourth day of Christmas,
My true love sent to me
Four colly birds,
Three French hens,
Two turtle-doves, and
A partridge in a pear-tree.

Christmas days.

The fifth day of Christmas,
My true love sent to me
Five gold rings,
Four colly birds,
Three French hens,
Two turtle-doves, and
A partridge in a pear-tree.

The sixth day of Christmas,
My true love sent to me
Six geese a-laying,
Five gold rings,
Four colly birds,
Three French hens,
Two turtle-doves, and
A partridge in a pear-tree.

The seventh day of Christmas,
My true love sent to me
Seven swans a-swimming,
Six geese a-laying,

Christmas days.

Five gold rings,
Four colly birds,
Three French hens,
Two turtle-doves, and
A partridge in a pear-tree.

The eighth day of Christmas,
My true love sent to me
Eight maids a-milking,
Seven swans a-swimming,
Six geese a-laying,
Five gold rings,
Four colly birds,
Three French hens,
Two turtle-doves, and
A partridge in a pear-tree.

The ninth day of Christmas,
My true love sent to me
Nine drummers drumming,
Eight maids a-milking,

Christmas days.

Seven swans a-swimming,
Six geese a-laying,
Five gold rings,
Four colly birds,
Three French hens,
Two turtle-doves, and
A partridge in a pear-tree.

The tenth day of Christmas,
My true love sent to me
Ten pipers piping,
Nine drummers drumming,
Eight maids a-milking,
Seven swans a-swimming,
Six geese a-laying,
Five gold rings,
Four colly birds,
Three French hens,
Two turtle doves, and
A partridge in a pear-tree.

Christmas days.

The eleventh day of Christmas,
My true love sent to me
Eleven ladies dancing,
Ten pipers piping,
Nine drummers drumming,
Eight maids a-milking,
Seven swans a-swimming,
Six geese a-laying,
Five gold rings,
Four colly birds,
Three French hens,
Two turtle-doves, and
A partridge in a pear-tree.

The twelfth day of Christmas,
My true love sent to me
Twelve lords a-leaping,
Eleven ladies dancing,
Ten pipers piping,
Nine drummers drumming,
Eight maids a-milking,
Seven swans a-swimming,

Christmas days.

Six geese a-laying,
Five gold rings,
Four colly birds,
Three French hens,
Two turtle-doves, and
A partridge in a pear-tree.

Leg over Leg.

LEG over leg,
As the dog went to Dover;
When he came to a stile,
Jump! he went over.

*Sing, sing, what
shall I sing?*

SING, sing, what shall I sing?
The cat has ate the pudding-string!
Do, do, what shall I do?
The cat has bit it quite in two.

Fiddle-De-Dee.

FIDDLE-DE-DEE, fiddle-de-dee,
The fly shall marry the humble-
bee.
They went to the church, and married
was she,
The fly has married the humble-bee.

*There was an old
Soldier of Bister.*

THERE was an old soldier of Bister
Went walking one day with his
sister,
When a cow at one poke
Tossed her into an oak,
Before the old gentleman missed her.

Fiddle cum fee.

A CAT came fiddling out of a barn,
  With a pair of bagpipes under her

  arm;

She could sing nothing but fiddle cum

  fee,

The mouse has married the bumble-bee!

Pipe, cat; dance, mouse:

We'll have a wedding at our good house.

Intery, mintery, cutery-corn.

INTERY, mintery, cutery-corn,
  Apple seed and apple thorn;

  Wine, brier, limber-lock,

  Five geese in a flock,

  Sit and sing by a spring,

  O-U-T, and in again.

As I was going to St. Ives.

AS I was going to St. Ives
  I met a man with seven wives;
Each wife had seven sacks,
In each sack were seven cats,
And each cat had seven kits.
Kits, cats, sacks, and wives,
How many were going to St. Ives?

Jack and Jill.

JACK and Jill went up the hill,
    To fetch a pail of water;
Jack fell down and broke his crown,
    And Jill came tumbling after.

Tom, Tom, the Piper's Son.

TOM, Tom, the piper's son,
    Stole a pig, and away he run;
The pig was eat and Tom was beat,
And Tom ran crying down the street.

Let us go to the Woods.

"LET us go to the woods," says Richard to Robin,

"Let us go to the woods," says Robin to Bobbin,

"Let us go to the woods," says John all alone,

"Let us go to the woods," says every one.

"What to do there?" says Richard to Robin,

"What to do there?" says Robin to Bobbin,

"What to do there?" says John all alone,

"What to do there?" says every one.

"We will shoot a wren," says Richard to Robin,

"We will shoot a wren," says Robin to Bobbin,

Let us go to the Woods.

"We will shoot a wren," says John all
alone,

"We will shoot a wren," says every one.

"Then pounce, pounce," says Richard to
Robin,

"Then pounce, pounce," says Robin to
Bobbin,

"Then pounce, pounce," says John all
alone,

"Then pounce, pounce," says every one.

"She is dead, she is dead," says Richard
to Robin,

"She is dead, she is dead," says Robin to
Bobbin,

"She is dead, she is dead," says John all
alone,

"She is dead, she is dead," says every one.

Let us go to the Woods.

"How shall we get her home?" says Richard to Robin,

"How shall we get her home?" says Robin to Bobbin,

"How shall we get her home?" says John all alone,

"How shall we get her home?" says every one.

"In a cart with six horses," says Richard to Robin,

"In a cart with six horses," says Robin to Bobbin,

"In a cart with six horses," says John all alone,

"In a cart with six horses," says every one.

"How shall we get her dressed?" says Richard to Robin,

Let us go to the Woods.

"How shall we get her dressed?" says
Robin to Bobbin,

"How shall we get her dressed?" says
John all alone,

"How shall we get her dressed?" says
every one.

"We will hire seven cooks," says Richard
to Robin,

"We will hire seven cooks," says Robin
to Bobbin,

"We will hire seven cooks," says John all
alone,

"We will hire seven cooks," says every
one.

Robin-a-Bobbin.

ROBIN-A-BOBBIN
Bent his bow,
Shot at a pigeon,
And killed a crow.

Old Woman, old Woman.

OLD woman, old woman, shall we go
a-shearing?

Speak a little louder, sir,—I am very
thick of hearing.

Old woman, old woman, shall I love you
dearly?

Thank you, kind sir. I hear you very
clearly.

The King of France,
and the King of Spain.

THE King of France, with twenty
thousand men,

Went up the hill, and then came down
again.

The King of Spain, with twenty thousand more,

Climbed the same hill the French had
climbed before.

185

Old Mother Hubbard.

OLD Mother Hubbard,
She went to the cupboard,
    To give her poor dog a bone,
But when she came there
The cupboard was bare,
    And so the poor dog had none.

She went to the baker's
    To buy him some bread,
And when she came back
    The poor dog was dead.

She went to the joiner's
    To buy him a coffin,
And when she came back
    The poor dog was laughing.

She took a clean dish
    To get him some tripe,
And when she came back
    He was smoking his pipe.

She went to the ale-house
    To get him some beer,
And when she came back
    The dog sat in a chair.

Old Mother Hubbard.
Page 186

Old Mother Hubbard.
Page 186

Old Mother Hubbard.
Page 186

Old Mother Hubbard.
Page 187

Old Mother Hubbard.

She went to the tavern
 For white wine and red,
And when she came back
 The dog stood on his head.

She went to the hatter's
 To buy him a hat,
And when she came back
 He was feeding the cat.

She went to the barber's
 To buy him a wig,
And when she came back
 He was dancing a jig.

She went to the fruiterer's
 To buy him some fruit,
And when she came back
 He was playing the flute.

She went to the tailor's
 To buy him a coat,
And when she came back
 He was riding a goat.

Old Mother Hubbard.

She went to the cobbler's
To buy him some shoes,
And when she came back
He was reading the news.

She went to the sempstress
To buy him some linen,
And when she came back
The dog was spinning.

She went to the hosier's
To buy him some hose,
And when she came back
He was dressed in his clothes.

The dame made a curtsey,
The dog made a bow;
The dame said, "Your servant,"
The dog said, "Bow, wow!"

Old Mother Hubbard.
Page 187

Old Mother Hubbard.
Page 187

Old Mother Hubbard.
Page 187

Old Mother Hubbard.
Page 188

Old Mother Hubbard.
Page 188

Hickety, Pickety.
Page 189

Lucy Locket.

LUCY LOCKET lost her pocket,
  Kitty Fisher found it;

Never a penny was there in it,
  Save the binding round it.

Hickety, Pickety.

HICKETY, pickety, my black hen,
  She lays eggs for gentlemen;
Gentlemen come every day
To see what my black hen doth lay.

189

Little brown Mouse.

PRETTY John Watts,
   We are troubled with rats,
Will you drive them out of the house?
   We have mice, too, in plenty,
   That feast in the pantry;
   But let them stay,
   And nibble away:
What harm in a little brown mouse?

Pussy-cat sits by the fire.

PUSSY-CAT sits by the fire:
   How did she come there?
In walks the little dog—
   Says, "Pussy! are you there?
How do you do, Mistress Pussy?
   Mistress Pussy, how d'ye do?"
"I thank you kindly, little dog,
   I fare as well as you!"

Pussy-cat sits by the fire.
Page 190

I had a little Dog.
Page 191

I had a little Dog.

I HAD a little dog, and his name
was Blue Bell,
I gave him some work, and he did it very
well;
I sent him upstairs to pick up a pin,
He stepped in the coal-scuttle up to the
chin;

I sent him to the garden to pick some
sage,
He tumbled down and fell in a rage;
I sent him to the cellar to draw a pot of
beer,
He came up again and said there was
none there.

Great A, little a.

GREAT A, little a, bouncing B,
The cat's in the cupboard and she
can't see.

Jenny Wren.

TWAS once upon a time
        When Jenny Wren was young,
So daintily she danced,
    And so prettily she sung;
Robin Redbreast lost his heart,
    For he was a gallant bird;
So he doffed his hat to Jenny Wren,
    Requesting to be heard.

O dearest Jenny Wren,
    If you will but be mine,
You shall feed on cherry pie, you shall,
    And drink new currant wine;
I'll dress you like a goldfinch,
    Or any peacock gay;
So dearest Jen, if you'll be mine,
    Let us appoint the day.

Jenny Wren.

Jenny blushed behind her fan,
　　And thus declared her mind:
Since, dearest Bob, I love you well,
　　I'll take your offer kind;
Cherry pie is very nice,
　　And so is currant wine;
But I must wear my plain brown gown
　　And never go too fine.

Robin Redbreast rose up early,
　　All at the break of day,
And he flew to Jenny Wren's house,
　　And sung a roundelay;
He sung of Robin Redbreast
　　And little Jenny Wren,
And when he came unto the end,
　　He then began again.

The Fox and his Wife.

THE fox and his wife they had a
  great strife,
They never ate mustard in all their whole
  life;
They ate their meat without fork or knife,
  And loved to be picking a bone, e-ho!

The fox jumped up on a moonlight night;
The stars they were shining, and all
  things bright;
Oh, ho! said the fox, it's a very fine night
  For me to go through the town, e-ho!

The fox when he came to yonder stile,
He lifted his lugs and he listened awhile!
Oh, ho! said the fox, it's but a short mile
  From this unto yonder wee town, e-ho!

The fox when he came to the farmer's
  gate,
Who should he see but the farmer's drake;
I love you well for your master's sake
  And long to be picking your bone, e-ho!

The Fox and his Wife.

The grey goose she ran round the hay-
stack,
Oh, ho! said the fox, you are very fat;
You'll grease my beard and ride on my
back
From this into yonder wee town, e-ho!

Old Gammer Hipple-hopple hopped out
of bed,
She opened the casement, and popped out
her head;
Oh! husband, oh! husband, the grey goose
is dead,
And the fox is gone through the town,
oh!

Then the old man got up in his red cap,
And swore he would catch the fox in a
trap;
But the fox was too cunning, and gave
him the slip,
And ran through the town, the town,
oh!

The Fox and his Wife.

When he got to the top of the hill,
He blew his trumpet both loud and shrill,
For joy that he was safe
    Through the town, oh!

When the fox came back to his den,
He had young ones both nine and ten,
"You're welcome home, daddy; you may
    go again,
If you bring us such nice meat
    From the town, oh!"

I had a little Hen.

I HAD a little hen, the prettiest ever
    seen,
She washed up the dishes, and kept the
    house clean;
She went to the mill to fetch me some
    flour,
She brought it home in less than an hour;
She baked me my bread, she brewed me
    my ale,
She sat by the fire and told me a fine tale.

Monday alone.

MONDAY alone,
Tuesday together,
Wednesday we walk
When it's fine weather.
Thursday we kiss,
Friday we cry,
Saturday's hours
Seem almost to fly.
But of all days in the week
We will call
Sunday, the rest day,
The best day of all.

There was an old Woman.

THERE was an old woman had three
          sons,
Jerry and James and John:
Jerry was hung, James was drowned,
John was lost, and never was found;
And there was an end of her three sons,
Jerry and James and John!

Little Tommy Tucker.

LITTLE Tommy Tucker,
Sing for your supper:
What shall I eat?
White bread and butter.
How shall I cut it
Without any knife?
How shall I marry
Without any wife?

The Piper and his Cow.

THERE was a Piper had a Cow,
And he had naught to give her;
He pulled out his pipes and played her a
tune,
And bade the cow consider.

The Cow considered very well,
And gave the Piper a penny,
And bade him play the other tune:
"Corn rigs are bonny."

I have been to Market.

I HAVE been to market, my lady,
   my lady.
Then you've not been to the fair, says

pussy, says pussy.
I bought me a rabbit, my lady, my lady.
Then you did not buy a hare, says pussy,

says pussy.

As white as Milk.

AS white as milk,
   And not milk;
      As green as grass,
      And not grass;
      As red as blood,
      And not blood;
      As black as soot,
      And not soot!

(*A bramble blossom.*)

199

Ride a Cock-horse
to Banbury Cross.

RIDE a cock horse to Banbury Cross
To see what Tommy can buy;
A penny white loaf, a penny white cake,
And a two-penny apple pie.

Mary, Mary, quite contrary.

MARY, Mary, quite contrary,
How does your garden grow?
Silver bells and cockle shells
And pretty maids all in a row.

JACK, be nimble,
Jack, be quick."
Jack ran off with the pudding-stick.

Taffy was a Welshman.

TAFFY was a Welshman, Taffy was
a thief,
Taffy came to my house and stole a leg
of beef;
I went to Taffy's house, Taffy wasn't
home;
Taffy came to my house and stole a mar-
row bone.
I went to Taffy's house, Taffy was in
bed;
I took the marrow-bone and beat Taffy's
head.

I'll tell you a Story.

I'LL tell you a story
About Mary Morey,
And now my story's begun.
I'll tell you another,
About her brother,
And now my story's done.

There was an old Woman
tossed up in a Basket.

THERE was an old woman tossed up
in a basket,
Seventy times as high as the moon.
What she did there I could not but ask
it,
For in her hand she carried a broom.

"Old woman, old woman, old woman,"
said I,
"Oh whither, oh whither, oh whither so
high?"
"To sweep the cobwebs off the sky,
And I shall be back again by and by."

There was a little Man.

THERE was a little man and he had
a little gun,
And his bullets were made of lead,
He shot John Sprig through the middle
of his wig,
And knocked it right off his head.

202

I had a little Hen.
Page 196

*There was an old Woman
tossed up in a Basket.*
Page 202

There was a crooked Man.

THERE was a crooked man, and he
went a crooked mile;

He found a crooked sixpence against a
crooked stile;

He bought a crooked cat, which caught a
crooked mouse;

And they all lived together in a little
crooked house.

Dickery, dickery, dare.

DICKERY, dickery, dare,
The pig flew up in the air;

The man in brown soon brought him
down,

Dickery, dickery, dare.

Daffy-down-dilly.

DAFFY-DOWN-DILLY is new
　　come to town,
With a petticoat green and a bright yel-
　　low gown.

Pease Porridge hot.

PEASE porridge hot,
Pease porridge cold,
　　Pease porridge in the pot
　　Nine days old.

Little Nancy Etticoat.

LITTLE Nancy Etticoat
In a white petticoat
And a red nose;
The longer she stands
The shorter she grows.

Hey, diddle, diddle.
Page 205

Hey, diddle, diddle.
Page 205

To Market, to Market.

TO market, to market,
To buy a penny bun.
Home again, home again,
Market is done.

The Man in the Moon.

THE man in the moon came down too
    soon,
And asked his way to Norwich;
He went by the south and burnt his
    mouth
With eating cold plum-porridge.

Hey, diddle, diddle.

HEY, diddle, diddle!
    The cat and the fiddle;
The cow jumped over the moon.
    The little dog laughed
    To see such craft;
And the dish ran away with the spoon.

Peter, Peter, Pumpkin Eater.

PETER, Peter, Pumpkin Eater,
Had a wife and couldn't keep her.
He put her in a pumpkin shell,
And there he kept her very well.

Peter, Peter, Pumpkin Eater,
Had another and didn't love her.
Peter learned to read and spell,
And then he loved her very well.

That's all.

THERE was an old man,
And he had a calf,
And that's half;
He took him out of the stall,
And put him on the wall;
And that's all.

206

Peter, Peter, Pumpkin Eater.

207

Hickory, dickory, dock.

HICKORY, dickory, dock;

The mouse ran up the clock;

The clock struck one,

The mouse ran down,

Hickory, dickory, dock.

There was an old Woman
sold Puddings and Pies.

THERE was an old woman

Sold puddings and pies;

She went to the mill,

And the dust flew in her eyes.

Now through the streets,

To all she meets,

She ever cries,

"Hot pies—Hot pies!"

Three Men in a Tub.

HEY, rub-a-dub-dub, three men in a
tub,
And who do you think were there?
The butcher, the baker, the candlestick
maker,
And all had come from the fair.

*Oh, dear, what can
the Matter be?*

OH, dear, what can the matter be?
Two old women got up in an apple-
tree;
One came down,
And the other stayed till Saturday.

Bow, wow, wow.

BOW, wow, wow,
Whose dog art thou?
Little Tom Tinker's dog,
Bow, wow, wow.

There was a mad Man.

THERE was a mad man,
    And he had a mad wife,
And they lived all in a mad lane.
They had three children all at a birth,
And they too were mad every one.
The father was mad,
The mother was mad,
The children all mad beside;
And upon a mad horse they all of them
        got,
And madly away did ride.

A Swarm of Bees.

A SWARM of bees in May
    Is worth a load of hay;
    A swarm of bees in June
    Is worth a silver spoon;
    A swarm of bees in July
    Is not worth a fly.

Higgledy, Piggledy.

HIGGLEDY, piggledy, my black hen,
She lays eggs for gentlemen;
Sometimes nine, and sometimes ten,
Higgledy, piggledy, my black hen.

Is John Smith within?

IS John Smith within?
Yes, that he is.
Can he set a shoe?
Ay, marry, two.
Here a nail, there a nail,
Now your horse is shoed.

*There was an
old Man of Tobago.*

THERE was an old man of Tobago,
Who lived on rice, gruel, and sago;
Till, much to his bliss,
His physician said this—
" To a leg, sir, of mutton you may go."

Diddle-y-diddle-y-dumpty.

DIDDLE-y-diddle-y-dumpty,
The cat run up the plum-tree,
Half-a-crown
To fetch her down,
Diddle-y-diddle-y-dumpty.

I will sing you a Song.

I WILL sing you a song,
Though 'tis not very long,
Of the woodcock and the sparrow,
Of the little dog that burned his tail,
And he shall be whipped to-morrow.

THERE was a girl in our towne,
Silk an' satin was her gowne,
Silk an' satin, gold an' velvet,
Guess her name—three times I've tell'd
it.   (*Ann.*)

Rock-a-bye, baby.

ROCK-A-BYE, baby, thy cradle is
    green;
Father's a nobleman, mother's a queen;
And Betty's a lady, and wears a gold
    ring;
And Johnny's a drummer, and drums for
    the king.

Cold and raw.

COLD and raw the north wind doth
    blow,
Bleak in a morning early;
All the hills are covered with snow,
    And winter's now come fairly.

Elizabeth.

ELIZABETH, Eliza, Betsy, and
    Bess,
Went over the water to rob a bird's nest,
They found a nest with five eggs in it,
They each took one, and left four in it.

My Mammy's Maid.

DINGTY, diddledy, my mammy's
  maid,
She stole oranges, I'm afraid;
Some in her pockets, some in her sleeve,
She stole oranges, I do believe.

A little old Man
and I fell out.

A LITTLE old man and I fell out:
   How shall we bring this matter
      about?
Bring it about as well as you can—
Get you gone, you little old man!

See a Pin
and pick it up.

SEE a pin and pick it up,
   All the day you'll have good luck;
   See a pin and let it lay,
   Bad luck you'll have all the day.

So, merrily trip and go.

TRIP and go, heave and ho!
Up and down, to and fro;
From the town to the grove,
Two and two let us rove,
A-maying, a-playing;
Love hath no gainsaying!
So, merrily trip and go!
So, merrily trip and go!

Brow brinky.

BROW brinky,
Eye kinky,
Chin choppy,
Nose noppy,
Cheek cherry,
Mouth merry.

I like little Pussy.

I LIKE little pussy, her coat is **so**
    warm,—
And if I don't hurt her she'll do me **no**
    harm;
I'll not pull her tail, nor drive her away,
But pussy and I very gently will play.

Come hither, sweet Robin.

COME hither, sweet robin,
    And be not afraid,
  I would not hurt even a feather;
Come hither, sweet Robin,
    And pick up some bread,
  To feed you this very cold weather.

I don't mean to frighten you,
    Poor little thing,
  And pussy-cat is not behind me;
So hop about pretty,
    And drop down your wing,
  And pick up some crumbs,
    And don't mind me.

Hey-ding-a-ding.

HEY-DING-A-DING! I heard a
    bird sing;
The parliament soldiers are gone to the
  king.

Cou'd ye?

I WOULD if I cou'd,
If I cou'dn't how cou'd I?

I cou'dn't, without I cou'd, cou'd I?

Cou'd you, without you cou'd, cou'd ye?

Cou'd ye, cou'd ye?

Cou'd you, without you cou'd, cou'd ye?

Ride, Baby, ride.

RIDE, baby, ride,
Pretty baby shall ride,

And have a little puppy-dog tied to her
side,

And little pussy-cat tied to the other,

And away she shall ride to see her grandmother,

To see her grandmother,

To see her grandmother.

In a Cottage in Fife.

IN a cottage in Fife
Lived a man and his wife,
Who, believe me, were comical folk;
For to people's surprise,
They both saw with their eyes,
And their tongues moved whenever they
spoke!

When quite fast asleep,
I've been told that, to keep
Their eyes open they scarce could con-
trive:
They walked on their feet,
And 'twas thought what they eat
Helped, with drinking, to keep them
alive!

One misty, moisty Morning.

ONE misty moisty morning,
When cloudy was the weather,
I chanced to meet an old man
Clothed all in leather.

He began to compliment,
And I began to grin;
How do you do, and how do you do?
And how do you do again?

ALL of a row,
Bend the bow,
Shot at a pigeon,
And killed a crow.

Where are you going?

"WHERE are you going, my pretty
    maid?"
"I'm going a-milking, sir," she said.
"May I go with you, my pretty maid?"
"You're kindly welcome, sir," she said.
"What is you father, my pretty maid?"
"My father's a farmer, sir," she said.
"What is your fortune, my pretty
    maid?"
"My face is my fortune, sir," she said.
"Then I can't marry you, my pretty
    maid!"
"Nobody asked you, sir!" she said.

Hot-cross Buns!

HOT-CROSS Buns!
    Hot-cross Buns!
One a penny, two a penny
    Hot-cross Buns!
    Hot-cross Buns!
    Hot-cross Buns!
If ye have no daughters,
    Give them to your sons.

*This is the death of
little Jenny Wren.*

THIS is the death of
      Little Jenny Wren,
And what the doctors
      All said then.

Jenny Wren was sick again,
      And Jenny Wren did die;
The doctors vowed they'd cure her,
      Or know the reason why.

Doctor Hawk felt her pulse,
      And, shaking his head,
Said, "I fear I can't save her,
      Because she's quite dead."

Doctor Hawk's a clever fellow,
He pinched her wrist enough to kill her.

"She'll do very well yet,"
      Then said Doctor Fox,
"If she takes but one pill
      From out of this box."

As I was going along, long, long.

AS I was going along, long, long,
    A-singing a comical song, song,
      song,
The lane that I went was so long, long,
    long,
And the song that I sung was as long,
    long, long,
And so I went singing along.

As I went through the Garden Gap.

AS I went through the garden gap,
    Who should I meet but Dick Red-
      cap!
A stick in his hand, a stone in his throat:
If you'll tell me this riddle, I'll give you
    a groat.

                  (*A cherry.*)

Long legs, crooked thighs,
Little head, and no eyes.

              (*Pair of tongs.*)

Dance to your Daddy.

DANCE to your daddy,
  My little babby,
  Dance to your daddy,
  My little lamb.

  You shall have a fishy
  In a little dishy;
  You shall have a fishy
  When the boat comes in.

There was an old woman of Leeds.

THERE was an old woman of Leeds
  Who spent all her time in good
    deeds;
  She worked for the poor
  Till her fingers were sore,
  This pious old woman of Leeds!

Why is Pussy in bed, pray?

WHY is pussy in bed, pray?
She is sick, says the fly,
And I fear she will die;
That's why she's in bed.

Pray, what's her disorder?
She's got a locked jaw,
Says the little jackdaw,
And that's her disorder.

Who makes her gruel?
I, says the horse,
For I am her nurse,
And I make her gruel.

Pray, who is her doctor?
Quack, quack! says the duck,
I that task undertook,
And I am her doctor.

Who thinks she'll recover?
I, says the deer,
For I did last year:
So I think she'll recover.

225

My little old Man and I fell out.

MY little old man and I fell out,
  I'll tell you what 'twas all about:
I had money, and he had none,
And that's the way the row begun.

Tommy Trot, a Man of Law.

TOMMY TROT, a man of law,
  Sold his bed and lay upon straw,—
Sold the straw and slept on grass,
To buy his wife a looking-glass.

Doodle doodle doo.

DOODLE doodle doo,
  The Princess lost her shoe;
Her Highness hopped,—
The fiddler stopped,
Not knowing what to do.

I had a little Husband.

I HAD a little husband
No bigger than my thumb,
I put him in a pint pot,
And there I bid him drum.

I bought a little horse,
That galloped up and down;
I bridled him, and saddled him,
And sent him out of town.

I gave him some garters,
To garter up his hose,
And a little handkerchief,
To wipe his pretty nose.

If "ifs" and "ands"
Were pots and pans,
There would be no need for tinkers!

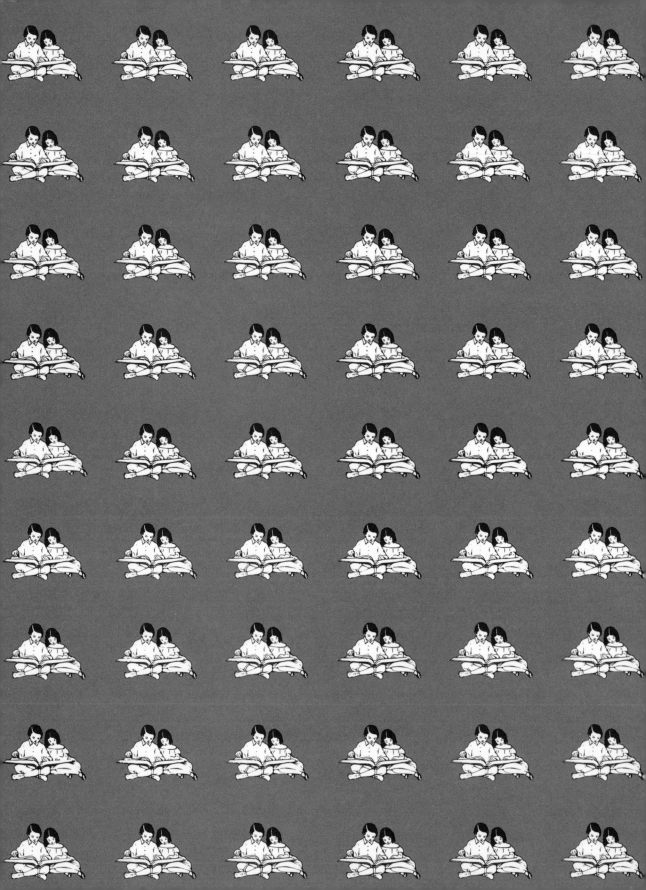